Celeste Blue

Lou Nell Gerard

Contents

Fixies Adrift

Originally published in Toasted Cheese June 1, 2014.

Autumn

The white pelican thought little about the two bodies slipping into the water and floating away through the canoe path between the sedge reeds. As long as they stayed clear of his school of rainbow trout he cared not about the activities of these wingless land creatures. He was working fast packing away fish before those double crested cormorants showed up.

Winter

"I still say that is an odd shape for reeds, seems too solid somehow."

"Well, feel free to head out on that ice to check it out...your snowshoes might help keep you from breaking through."

"It might just be thick enough this year, but then so am I, thick this year...naaaww...we'll see come Spring."

"Thank you."

"Huh?"

"Thick...you're thick because of my irresistible cooking, right? Don't tell me that wasn't a compliment."

Spring

Reeds shed their winter snow hoar leaving shining wet and brilliant green against cerulean blue.

Lois and Lonny were enjoying their shore walk sans snowshoes. Soon they'd be bringing the canoe down to its fair-weather dock they shared with the summer folk.

"Look at that heron with pink feet!"

"Herons don't have pink feet. Grey, kind of a yellow orangey color I think, maybe black. No, no pink feet. You've got that pink-toed tarantula on your mind. It must be standing on something pink. What is it standing on?"

"What do you mean? I'm talking about that one there in the reeds."

"No no no...look at it. I mean yes, I know you are talking about the one in the reeds. Look, that's that spot, that odd shape we saw in the snow all winter long. There is something there in the reeds. That heron is standing on something pink."

"Let's go get the canoe."

Raft

As they approached the reeds they squinted and strained to try to justify some of the odd angles and colors they were seeing in the reeds, finally as they slipped through one of the old canoe channels they saw something pink, probably what the "pink-footed" heron was standing on. They nosed further in and there stood amongst the reeds two bicycles, one of them with a pink saddle. The bikes were aboard a rather substantial raft. Using their lines, they fashioned a loop around a corner of the raft and given that there wasn't much movement of the lake water in this little bay they felt secure stepping aboard the raft, after all it had wintered over there. This then was the "odd shape for reeds" they'd debated about. They felt like children, the both of them, who've found a great discovery. One bike was a black Bianchi fixed gear bike, the other, also a Bianchi "fixie", sort of a turquoise blue-ish color called "Celeste" they were to learn later. The latter was the one with the pink saddle.

Wonder and excitement alight on their faces they felt as though they were getting a tour of a stage set.

"Fixies on a raft...out here...and look at all the rest!"

"All the rest" included a picnic basket still propped open and lined with a blue, yellow, and white checked waffle fabric dish towel. There was a quarter-empty jar of pickled walnuts, shreds from a box of some sort—maybe crackers, and a red wax half-shell full of beak marks that very likely came off a cheese. There was a small ceramic knife and a bamboo five-inch by eight-inch oil stained cutting board and an empty sardine can. Of course, nothing edible remained whether dined on by humans or devoured by lake dwellers was unclear although the dish towel did have some distinctly beak like marks and was in a bit of disarray. Perhaps cormorants and otters got together and dined on the raft, was heron invited? Ducks? Centered on the raft the fixies held by portable triangle stands, created an enclosure like that of a small sidewalk wrought iron fence. This framed a small light outdoor cafe table and two matching chairs. A floral muslin shawl draped over the back of one chair had slipped and was hanging as if placed "off-the-shoulder" of the chair. It was a delicate creation of pale greens and blues and yellows and pinks, flowers and vines on a cream background. Part of the shawl draped itself on the rough-hewn timber of the raft—the corner just dipped into the water as if taking a sip. On the table, an empty bottle of 2009 RoxyAnn Viognier, two crystal wine glasses one of them still bore pink lip prints overlapped as though the drinker rotated the glass to drink from a lipstick free rim with each sip, and two bamboo fiber and melamine plates in a bright Mediterranean pattern. Lois thought immediately how odd to contrast the delicate breakable crystal wine flutes with the practical but still quite lovely plates. Tucked under the wine bottle was a piece of heavy paper. It looked as though it had a sketch of some kind on it, but the melting snow had left simply a pattern of washed colors, had that been a blue elephant? Letters of some kind?

Thirty-eight degrees, still cold even in the full blast of early Spring sun. Everything about the scene sparkled, even the rough-hewn timbers of the raft itself, still wet from snow melt glistened. Under each chair a pair of shoes sat as neatly as if on display. The shawl-draped chair guarded a pair of Jimmy Choo sandals with a spiked four-inch heel, pale green, size 8. No scuff marks but worn enough that part of the 'JIM' of the label on the footbed was slightly faded from friction. Later investigation revealed them to be from Jimmy Choo's 2014 line. 'Lance' sandals in Peppermint retailing for around $775.00. These shoes had not been in contact with a bike pedal of any kind. Facing directly, as though in conversation with the sandals were a well-worn pair of Converse Chuck Taylor "Year of the Dragon" men's high tops, no laces, size 13. Probably retailed in 2012 for around $90.00. This particular pair did not have an 'original owner' look about them. Later close inspection revealed that the footbed was worn in two distinctly different pressure patterns. The bottoms as well were worn both like they were worn by a pronator and supinator, and they bore a look of having once been laced frequently.

The table was set with a pale yellow linen tablecloth, a lapis blue linen napkin was wadded up to the left of the plate belonging to the high tops and the matching napkin was draped across the seat of the Jimmy Choo chair, a silver fork rested tines down at three o'clock on the empty dinner plate. Next to this plate was a tube of Laura Mercier 'Spring Renaissance' Crème Smooth Lip Color, Palm Beach lipstick, still sitting upright as improbable as that may seem. Lois reached for the tube, then caught herself just as she was about to pick it up. Luckily, enthralled as they were, they had not yet handled anything.

On the raft itself in the corner opposite the picnic basket sat a Crosley Echo portable battery-operated turntable in a retro red and cream case. One vinyl had been playing: Billie Holiday's *All or Nothing at All,* 1958 on Verve records. Still in their cardboard album sleeves sat: Miles Davis's *Kind of Blue,* 1959 on Columbia Records and

Ascenseur pour l'échafaud, 1958 on the Fontana label along with John Coltrane's *Ballads,* 1961 on Impulse! Records. Tucked between the portable turntable and the albums propped against the side of the lid was a slim, folded cane. A white reflective cane used by someone who is blind. Magic and wonder gave way to gravity. Two bicycles, one cane. Lonny had been in a marathon once with a runner who was blind, she had a runner guide...could that work for a bike? He just couldn't visualize it...well of course, but...

This, the cane more than anything, the bikes, the shoes, the emptiness of the picnic basket sent a chill up Lois's spine. Lois looked at Lonny and they both reached for their phones with grim faces. Adventure and discovery had given way to a feeling neither of them could describe. That feeling when there seems no ready explanation, when time slows and life sounds like the lapping water against the raft, soft wind through the reeds, the quiet bark of the canoe against the raft, bird song the occasional splash of a fish or a landing lake bird all disappears and is replaced by a tone of the imagination much like the deep deep tonals of the throat singing monks of Tibet. Seeing each other pulling their phones out they each started to demure. Then they compared signal strength and his phone "won" or maybe "lost" so Lonny made the 911 call.

"Sir, please don't touch anything else and get off the raft. Can you paddle to Harbinger's landing and meet the sheriff to guide him and his team out?"

The sheriff's department launch idled along trying not to overtake the canoe, Deputy June Wolmar was wishing she had her pole and line to string along behind...why not grab some trout on duty? She and the sheriff were both fit with winter-tan faces, both wore Ray Ban aviator sunglasses, June's with brown tint, what she called "happy glass" Dan's with a dark grey-green tint...she always found that tint depressing while her brown tint added a golden light.

Everyone was quiet, seeming to enjoy the sun, the quiet purr and sputter of the barely idling outboard, the light splashes of the oars, the occasional knock of an oar against the canoe...winter had de-conditioned both Lonny and Lois from paddling smoothly.

When they reached the raft Deputy Wolmar dropped the bow anchor and took a few pictures with her phone then nodding to the sheriff, she and Sheriff Dan Markham stepped aboard the raft. Markham called in the forensics team who had been on standby in case of hoax or false alarm. He asked them to arrange for divers too. The team would use GPS to locate and join them. Then he pulled out a pocket spiral notepad and mechanical pencil. Wolmar had grabbed her iPad out of a pack she had thrown on board the launch. They worked well together though their choice of tools was different. Almost back to back, they slow waltzed around each other in silence taking a full three-hundred sixty-degree view of the scene before starting to take notes. Wolmar periodically used her iPad to take pictures, Markham knew he didn't have to direct her, she was methodical and thorough, some people said she was "OCD" as though it were a precursor to the plague or something, well, fine he thought, all the better for my team.

Lois and Lonny weren't sure if they were in the way, dismissed or witnesses so they sat rather uncomfortably in the canoe and shrugged their shoulders at each other. It was getting cold now that they weren't moving. After about fifteen minutes Lonny cleared his throat.

"Oh, sorry, can you give the deputy here your names and phone numbers then you can go for now, we'll be contacting you later...and please keep this to yourselves?"

"Well they certainly didn't come out here in the winter..." June was crouched down admiring the Jimmy Choo sandals without touching them. "When was our last good picnic weather?"

"You are assuming that these people buckled to the types of choices we make—maybe they came out when it was already cold...well...we've had no rainfall in a record period, so I'll grant it was likely dry. Then snow, cold, snow and now melt. How long? How long?"

"Look here Dan, attached to the side here" June had located two punting poles and a paddle snapped into place by a pair of sideways mounted shovel and rake snap holders. "Where did they launch the raft? Did they stop here or drift here after, after whatever? It is a pretty spot."

"OK, let's do the list, not much more we can do until the forensics and divers arrive."

"The bikes, fairly new, expensive looking, they still have serial numbers. Purchased where, by whom, reported stolen?" June was a fast typist and easily frustrated by her voice capture tool, so she madly tapped away in Pages using her onscreen keyboard as they talked.

"What depths do those punting poles work in? Lake depth, can we backtrack and map possible paths for the raft? Any kind of current here, it is a big lake?"

"There are big sections where it'd be nearly impossible to get a raft that size to the lake, we can eliminate those and let's first focus here on Upper Lake. No candles or lantern, longer day? Oh! And the drawing."

"No signs of violence, but it looks so awfully like a stage set...that could mean nothing." Dan, in fact was thinking about street art but wasn't ready to say anything. This wasn't a city building or sidewalk that had been painted after all. This was remote, where was the audience...no, highly unlikely...it certainly would be an expensive temporary 'installation'.

"Or everything, everything..." June too was thinking of a stage set, a stage set by a perpetrator to make everything look "copacetic". That's the word he or she or them would use.

"Where are the clothes? Well, shoes left behind, but no little pile of clothes neatly stacked...it would fit wouldn't it?"

"Well, something unfortunate happened or someone had an

expensive little celebration and walked away, or swam or rowed or..."

"Or not."

Summer's End

Lois and Lonny walked and rowed almost every day through Spring and Summer. They often speculated about the raft. The Sheriff's department towed it away after a week's worth of in-place investigation. No information was forthcoming to the folks who found it. A brief flurry of local talk and headlines, then the biggest rainbow trout catches regained their rightful place.

June and Dan, unbeknownst to each other frequented the archive room, each looking for an overlooked clue. Each haunted by the questions and their own particular theories. Dan loved the idea of a stage manager or someone like that creating this set for whomever came across it to draw their own conclusions...sort of a three-dimensional Banksy for the great outdoors. In which case it was too bad the raft couldn't have stayed out there in the reeds for as long as the weather, otters, cormorants, herons, pelicans, ducks, woodpeckers, flickers and bugs let it stand. Of course, someone would have made off with the bikes and those Jimmy Choo's. June was of a less optimistic mind, but unclear as to details. Neither of them wanted this one to end up "Unsolved".

Derecho

Originally published in Toasted Cheese September 1, 2018.

Mile 1, Elise, Metro 295, Morning Dove Coffee

One of the new hybrids, sparkling and quiet, pulls into Transit Center Bay 4. It is early dawn and already hot, rather, still hot. There is a pneumatic puff as the doors open and cold air from the bus tumbles out, lost to the heat wave outside. Woven scents of soaps from all the morning showers descend and hang in the air as students bound for the community college, office workers, laborers, and night lifers step down off the bus.

Elise rolls her bike to the curb and waves at the driver. He gives her the thumbs up. She rolls it off the curb, lowers the bike rack, loads her bike on the front section, secures the support arm over the front wheel and moves into the queue, bus pass ready to scan.

She smooths the back of her skirt as she settles on one of the higher seats at the back of the first section of the articulated bus. She pulls out her iPad and balances it on the backpack in her lap. She leaves the seat next to her open anticipating a full commute into the university district, pill hill, then the downtown core. The pneumatic puff repeats as the doors close and the bus pulls away like a quiet dragon. The air conditioning works double-time to make up for the heat that boarded the bus like another passenger.

The deep blue sky is full of towers of cumulus clouds doing a quickstep march. They are positioned exactly where one of the local hot air balloon festivals takes place. She watches them sail quickly toward her. Her attention shifts as the kids bound for early university classes settle in with their energy bars, Odwalla drinks, and bloodshot eyes. A few pull out texts or tablets, most look hopeful for a few more winks. One is already curled up in a fetal position, her checkered canvas sneakers tucked on the seat, jungle red nails at the ends of her small delicate fingers cup her ankles. Her black knit watch cap implores "Love Me". She has a little pout painted red.

Back outside, the sky on the horizon has turned from deep blue to dark gray green and the cumulus clouds, racing in her direction bump into each other, flare out flat, and connect at the top. She hears something slide as the bus rounds a corner and brakes for the next stop. She looks down to see a bright pink toothbrush with green bristles slide out from under a seat. A woman's cane crashes to the floor. Across from her an Asian girl in black watch plaid skinny jeans and four-inch suede peach stilettos picks up the woman's cane for her. A wraith thin woman with a fever sheen to her face climbs on with heavy luggage. Elise wonders that she could lift it. She sits and a big shiver wracks her body. She digs out her cell phone and throws one leg atop her bag.

A woman sits down next to Elise. Her bench-mate's feet with Celeste Blue toenails swing freely in white leather flip flops. A flash of departing morning sun lights the chin of a passenger in a dragon tee and the forehead of another across the aisle with his Beats and his music. Nooks, Kindles, iPads, phones. The crackle of a couple of good old-fashioned newspapers, books. Watchers with smiles, with arms crossed bleary-eyed, with straight-ahead stares. The articulated center of the bus, the last seats to be filled, hosts a lanky boy with baggy trousers and a ball cap pulled down low.

There came a changing of the guard at the transit center. The new bench mate sits down on the flare of Elise's skirt. Thumbs still poised over his phone; one man sleeps through it all. Beats person reads the newspaper over another man's shoulder and the bus is now at standing room only. Elise watches the lake turn serious gunmetal gray green, reflecting the color of the horizon. Sunlight no longer makes its way past the bank of clouds which have formed an arched shelf. Low, dark, and menacing.

The couple across from Elise release hands as the man gets up for his stop. The woman, smiling a private smile, now holds her own hands on her lap as they pass into the dark of the tunnel.

The bus emerges from the tunnel to amplified crackling and an alarming jagged light. Another followed by two enormous booms reverberate Elise's insides. The clouds now form a ceiling, like the low dark roof of a sports dome, crack, crack, crack a series of lightning bolts is followed by the bellowing thunder.

In the seat in front of Elise little hands hang on the windowsill. A child's face, freckles pressed against the glass, head turning, laughing, pointing, smiling with joy, and speaking his own special language. His world goes by the window of the 295 and it is wonderful. His fellow passengers show mixed feelings, few share his enthusiasm, most of them have never seen a sky like this, some hope this means the end of the heat wave.

As Elise puts her iPad away and readies for her stop, the deluge begins, driven almost horizontal by the wind. "Great!" She's early for her meeting. She shrugs her shoulders. "Oh well." As she waits in line to get off the bus, she spots a place of refuge from the storm, Morning Dove Coffee, named after the Mourning Dove, but the proprietor feared the word mourning might steer some people clear of the premises. She isn't the only passenger planning a dash for the Morning Dove. She taps her bicycle helmet at the driver, and he gives her a nod and thumbs up. She removes her bike from the rack, lifts the rack back into place in record time. Soaked, she runs head down against the driving rain with her bike across the street and locks it on the bike rack near the entrance. She is not alone taking refuge in Morning Dove Coffee. It is packed with bedraggled folk; pools of rainwater are already gathering on the floor. Streaks of lightning crackle and thunder booms.

The screen over the baristas usually displays album art and info about the current song has been tuned to a news channel. A news anchor is interviewing a NOAA spokesperson who is standing in front of storm cloud diagrams, "…and can you explain why the extent of this thunderstorm, this um Derecho, was not predicted?"

"While typical thunderstorms are reasonably well-forecast, the complexity of a Derecho-producing storm system are not yet fully understood and observation networks…"

Elise orders a quad, no room.

Mile 325, Exit 18, Peg's, "Homemade Pies, Fresh Coffee All Day"

Peg carries the round tray full of plates of food as though it is an extension of her left arm. The coffee pot in her right hand, likewise, seems like part of her anatomy. Skinny as a rail, tough as they come.

"Ha ha ha, what Lucy don't know won't hurt ya Dan'l, fresh out of the oven this morning. Peach, loaded with cinnamon the way you like." Peg's smoker's voice can be heard from one end of the little crossroads café to the other.

"Come on go for it Dan'l, you know we're not squealers." Jolene, Daniel's cousin chimes in from the center of the café.

An impromptu barbershop quartet from the back corner starts up:

I dream of pie with the light brown crust

Baked by Peggy, with loving care

I dream of fresh peaches baked within

That crust of care and cinnamon

"All right already you clowns, but if Lucy finds out about this…" Daniel growls.

Peg, who knew her customers, already had Daniel's pie on her serving tray, she triumphantly places it in front of him, "There you go

Dan'l, I think this is one of my best yet, but you tell me." She sets the coffee pot down and puts her right hand on her cocked hip, waiting for his first bite. He cuts his first piece from the point, closes his eyes and makes a wish as he chews—a childhood habit. He chews dramatically slowly, "Hmmm, mmumph." He nods, opens his eyes swallows and reaches his arm around Peg's waist. "Darlin' they'll be serving this up in heaven." She nods, satisfied, picks up the coffee pot, tops his mug off and continues her rounds.

"Gettin' dark in here Peg, did ya pay the light bill?" Jeff asks from the counter where he likes to sit, the first stool but one.

Peg dips at the waist a little and peaks out a window, "Say, would ya look at that sky? Ain't seen a sky like that, since, nope, well, never like that…dark like that, but not that big…damn if it don't look like an alien spaceship dominating the sky like that. Well folks hope you aren't seeing' the end o' the world here in ole Peg's."

"I could think a worse places Peg, top off all our coffees, and how about pie all around since Dan'l says its good enough for heaven! Oh, and make it on the house. Har har har har."

"Now I just might to spite ya, Levi you old coot!"

The door opens and bangs and bounces as a gust pulls it out of the new customer's hand. The couple are probably travelers, no one knows them, but they are just as welcome as the regulars. Peg, still busy with serving says over her shoulder, "Sit anyplace you like, well except Johnie's table over there, she points with her chin at a table in the corner window. It has a single place setting, a poppy in a vase, a photo of a boy in uniform and a display of medals. Sitting on one of the windowsills is a US flag folded and displayed in a triangle.

"Say, what is this storm you've brought in folks?"

"We feel like it's been chasing us!" the woman says as she heads for a table toward the back. "Davey tells me not to worry so of course, now I'm really scared." Everyone in Peg's chuckles.

Davey grins, as he pulls out a chair for his wife, "Aw now Lois. Well, everybody, I don't believe I can take credit for this one. The radio is saying it is what's called a Derecho, like a giant, fast moving conga line of a storm. The thing is crossing state borders. Not very common especially this far west. From what I can gather we are maybe about in the middle of the thing. I guess over 250 miles is not uncommon. They say the North American record holder covered 1,300 miles. Yah, Minnesota, into southern Canada then headed out off the coast of Maine."

"Never heard of one, you Nosey?" Peg pours Clement "Nosey" Gray another cup.

"Not I, not I, Peg, cheers!" Nosey lifts his now full cup, nods at Peg then downs the hot brew in short order.

Outside the windows it looks like nighttime until a bolt of cloud-to-ground lighting lights up the sky and the café followed by a rolling thunder. Another streak of bright electric light reaches from above the clouds to the ground and rebounds back. Its thunder roar took less time to reach them. It felt like Peg's little café actually shook. Crack-crack, double-strike and a roaring rolling BOOM prompts sounds not dissimilar to the sounds made by crowds watching fireworks.

The lights flicker.

"Oh oh, get out yer zippos boys and gals, we're about to go down, glad we got the gas going in the kitchen already!"

The regulars pulled out lighters or matches, lifted the little glass globes from the candles in the center of their tables, lit the candles like it was common practice here. Davey and his partner Lois, non-smokers, look around. Jolene, at the adjacent table, passes them her lighter and Davey lights the candle, "Much obliged."

Mile 815, Holly, Code J45.901, Mostly Caff Café

Holly, a long-time barista at Mostly Caff, is now also interning as a pulmonologist at Mercy, the nearby university hospital. Very near—

across the street actually. Many of the customers at the Mostly Caff Café are in scrubs. She was advised to quit her day job as soon as her internship started but she is young and energetic and has her eye on an elite racing bicycle. Everyone told her she'd be consumed by exhaustion, but she decided to wait and see.

She likes working the café. There is something familiar and comforting about it. Even crowded. Somehow the blending of multiple, low conversations sounds like a loft full of messenger pigeons coo-coo cooo, coo-coo cooo. Then there are the regulars, many of them fellow students, she likes the contact.

She and Hank are an efficient duo with the shift change crowd. It is especially busy today with regulars and non-regulars. Today is a guest day. Easy to spot, the first group huddles rather than queues. Five of them all wearing visitors' badges around their upper arms like blood draw Coban. They are talking amongst themselves; she pegs them for the type that chat constantly as the line moves forward. She is right. They form a block oblivious to the people just trying to maneuver through the café. When it is their turn, they look almost shocked, the clump disperses as they peer into the cases of food and crane their necks to read the drink offerings. She smiles, right every time. Her eyes make contact with one of her regulars behind the group, they both shrug their shoulders, amused "What are ya gonna do?"

Holly had not seen the sky since arriving for work. Everyone coming in is describing it differently, but all agree it is like nothing they've ever seen before. Fast moving, a solid bank of low cumulus-like stuff, dark and menacing and heading their way. One person likened it to Birnam Woods' assault on Dunsinane. All she knows is that, her ears, particularly sensitive to pressure changes, are bothering her. Suddenly the already dim Mostly Caff becomes even darker, like blackout curtains had dropped, the way they do in the classroom prior to a video lesson. Just as sharply, darkness is broken as strobes, brilliant and revealing—almost blinding—

flash brightly and give the room the feel of an old gothic mansion in a bad horror film.

Soon a deluge is audible on the roof. More people pour into the already crowded café. Many, just off work decide to wait out the thunderstorm before catching their bus home. None of the bus shelters are adequate to the task of shielding people from this thing.

Pitched above the cracks of lightning and the rumbling of thunder comes the sound of aid cars. It is not unusual to hear sirens since the ER is just across the street, but it is unusual to hear so many so close together. Suddenly beepers, phones, and watch alerts are capturing the attention of almost everyone in the place, including Holly. She glances down at her watch and asks one of her co-workers who was about to leave, "Hey Rhond, can you um not leave? I have an emergency call, I gotta run over to Mercy."

Rhonda looked at her, shrugged back into her work apron by way of answer and muttered, "I won't say it…"

"Thanks, Rhond, I owe ya."

Over at Mercy, Holly is startled by the array of ambulance and aid cars. Inside she finds chaos instead of what is usually a well-oiled machine of efficiency. She recognizes at least three triage nurses with their hands full with so many patients looking "life threatening" or at least "urgent." She races through gurneys with people clearly in distress many with intubations and makeshift stations with oxygen bottles. She makes it to the locker area to jump into her scrubs. The locker room is more crowded than she's ever seen it.

"What's up Bec?"

"Just up your alley Holly, severe asthma attacks, some folks who've never experienced it before. The numbers…crazy. Almost like a fast-moving epidemic."

"An outburst of asthma attacks? Sure, it isn't some demented terrorist chemical attack?"

"Here? You watch too much news, kid. Hey Zack! They called you in too?"

Sandy, still in scrubs, who works in the office of the Unit Secretary pops in just to drop off his backpack and interjects, "Yep, they even called me back. I guess they'll want me pre-filling intake and charge forms. I already have it memorized. Code J45.901—asthma, unspecified, acute exacerbation.

"I think they are calling everyone in. I saw this when I was a paramedic in Melbourne." Zack is a resident. "Thunderstorm asthma. Lots of work done on this in Australia."

Holly, Bec, and Zack now into their scrubs continue their conversation as they rush down the hall to see where they are most needed.

"Come on Zack, this is no time for one of your down-under stories."

Zack continues. "No, straight. Lots of research done after several events including deaths. Theory is the violent activity of a thunderstorm breaks pollen grains into even finer particles than usual. The fragments or particles are so small they pass through the body's natural defenses and get into the lungs. That's why it gets some people who've never had asthma before and really does a number on asthma sufferers."

The charge nurse puts Holly on preparing salbutamol and adrenaline syringes, some for the ER, some to go out with the aid cars. Bec is sent to help set up more resuscitation beds. Zack is given his first patient, a terrified boy, already intubated, eyes wide, he clings to Zach's outstretched hand.

Eidolon

Originally published in Toasted Cheese March 1, 2019.

It was subtle. Re-routing her commutes to and from work. She considered her routing as a means to avoid road construction, school bus stops, garbage trucks on pick-up day, the mainstream uptight crazy traffic, or simply enjoy a scenic route. Of course, now that it was dark on her way to and from work, she couldn't rationalize "scenic" anymore. She considered being able to enjoy a full episode rather than mere snippets of Rufus Roundstone's *Noir In the 21st Century* as a side benefit of, rather than the reason for these extended commutes.

Beryl loved film noir but was often too tired after getting home from work to stay awake through a movie. A friend suggested podcasts during her commute. Beryl was skeptical. How could a podcast recreate lighting, Dutch angles, haunting tendrils of cigarette smoke—all essential in creating noir's ambience? Nevertheless, she decided to give it a try. She was surprised at the abundance of noir podcasts available. She tried a few but *Noir In the 21st Century* was the clear winner. Rufus Roundstone's voice was the voice of noir. Imagine a voice that combined the timbre and characteristics of James Earl Jones, Laurence Fishburne, and George Sanders. The content varied. Re-imagined classics (The Falcon, Marlowe, Spade), neo noir, interviews and special intros with the likes of Noir Czar Eddie Muller. Perfect.

She normally struggled against the onset of winter, but now she welcomed the drives in the dark and the rain. It helped make up for what she considered the limitations of audio only. The quiet metronome of her fore and aft windshield wipers blended with the foley work in the podcast. She was in her own private little theater complete with a heated seat. The extended trip home helped ease the transition to what she considered her weaker side. Beryl was an extremely talented designer and she knew it. At work she was strong, independent, decisive. Once "outside," in public, even at home, it all seemed to fall away, a Superhero stripped of her powers. She was prone to anxiety attacks. Decisions almost shut her down.

Hec had not noticed that Beryl arrived home later each day. First, that was Beryl, born fashionably late. Also, the seasonal switch flipped. The shorter days of winter made him feel perpetually late. Leaving work late, getting home late, eating dinner late. So, he dismissed Beryl rolling in after dark as part of his own perception of lateness. He wasn't overly alarmed—until their daughter asked,

"Hey dad. 'S'up with mom?"

"What do you mean Abb?"

"She's, well…" Abby looked around in an exaggerated manner, "um not home yet, right?"

"Abby, it's not that late, just your perception now that it's cold and gets dark early and…"

"And almost 9 o'the clock dad." She shoved her watch up under his nose.

Hec looked at Abby's watch. He checked his own. His face didn't match the reassuring words, "Ah, Abb, you know what a workaholic she can be. She's probably on some kind of a roll with this latest design project of hers."

"Ya well, she better not be late Thursday."

"What's Thursday?"

Abby made fish mouth and her eyes rolled, feeling her dad a little clueless, "Only their big annual gala party? The one we're invited to? The one where she's getting that surprise doo dah thing?"

As Hec watched his daughter's gestures he lamented to himself, "She's been watching too many teen sitcoms and melodramas."

"Right, right, right! They are giving her the Imagine Design Award. More than just a doo dah Abb. They don't give those out lightly. This is the first in five years."

The morning was dark with gusts of wind that rocked her Leaf a bit. The wind gathered the rain and pelted the car making percussive splashes. Perversely, by noon it was unseasonably sunny and warm. Beryl took advantage of the weather to run her car through the wash and vacuum it during her lunch break. She wanted to get in the habit of keeping it nice, and though still new, the dash had collected dust and she'd started to detect a faint, unpleasant odor. If she didn't know better, she'd say there'd been a smoker in the car. She shrugged her shoulders thinking, "Maybe a salesman or someone on a test drive? How rude. But then, why am I only just noticing it?" She shrugged.

She enjoyed the conveyer ride through the car wash, the rainbow-colored foam sprayed out and ran down the windows, the wax had a familiar and reassuring scent, and the jet blower sounded like a small jet engine starting up. The conveyer spit her and the Leaf out and she rolled across the lot to the quarter vacs. She wasn't the only one taking advantage of this unprecedented, balmy day. Beryl got out and admired her first new car. She'd chosen the Deep Blue Pearl exterior with black cloth, which was shot through with blue threads, a nice complement to the exterior color. She opened all doors, took out floor mats and hung them on the available clips. "That's odd," she thought as what looked like bits of cigarette ash floated out and off the front and back mats. She plopped her ziplock bag full of quarters near the coin slot, dropped several in and began to vacuum. She started whistling music from *The Barber of Seville*. She ended up singing lyrics from *The Rabbit of Seville*.

She had to use her fingernails to unweave some long blonde hairs from the cloth upholstery of the back seat. She frowned and tried to remember if she'd had anyone with hair that length and color in her car. Abby was the only one she remembered sitting in back and she had inherited the dark red hair of her mother. She shrugged and decided it must have been there from some other customer, maybe took the whole family on a test drive, maybe the smoker's family. "Still," she thought, "you'd think the detailers would have cleaned up better before handing over the keys."

The drive home that night was under a clear sky, but the coldest yet. As soon as the sun had set, the temperature dropped like a hammer blow. Beryl shivered as she felt the contrast of the cold with the rapidly warming seat. She pulled out of the parking lot and decided to take the route around the lake, then started episode 6.

The sound of rain, a car door thudded. Beryl swore she felt the car shift slightly. She wondered if the gusting winds of morning were returning. She imagined she smelled wet wool.

"OK so you found me Delilo, what's the score anyway?"

"You coulda shaken your hat off before getting in at least Dill, you used to be a gentleman."

"Well, this gentleman doesn't appreciate being strong-armed into a car, although I do appreciate being outta the rain and I thank you for that." Groan. "Where'd you get those guys anyway? A heavyweight two-for-one sale?"

"Distant cousins needed a leg up with employment."

"Does their parole officer know what they're doing?"

"Don't get cute Dill. You're no good at comedy. Got a little job for ya."

"I don't do your kinda job anymore Delilo, you know that, trying to stay on the straight and narrow."

"Yah well, do this one last job for me and we'll forget about that debt your wife is building up at my place. By the way try to keep her out OK? I've never seen a dame so unlucky. Kinda makes me feel sorry for her."

"You never felt sorry for anyone Delilo, not even yourself."

Sounds of shifting and a stubbled chin being scratched. She thought she smelled a faint scent of some aftershave, like something her grandfather used to wear. "Didn't realize I was so impressionable." Beryl grinned to herself, enjoying the added sensory experience her imagination was creating.

"It's an easy enough job for you Dill. Walk in the park." A wood match striking, the scent of cigarette smoke. "This dame's not even spilled milk, no one going to cry over her...passing. One of those spoiled rich dames likes to go slumming. Enemies in both camps. Cops want her on a murder rap."

"Let 'em have her."

"Uh uh. Knows something she shouldn't."

Beryl heard breathing, the sound of cigarette smoke being blown out—she could smell it, then it seemed a bit of smoke wafted into her peripheral vision. She felt the car shift a bit.

"So, the whole debt forgotten? Can, oh, what's his name..." a finger snap, "Biegler! He still your mouthpiece? Can he write up an agreement, call it an insurance policy for me that'll stick?"

"Biegler can do that in his sleep. But you gotta keep your wife outta my place, or let our bouncers keep her out. We usually keep the hands off the ladies."

A snort, "She's no lady. Not since she got that ring on her finger...sure had me bamboozled. Be my guest, toss her out, better yet, don't let her in. You know what she's like after a few drinks...or at least you oughtta. She is still your sister you know, or had you forgotten?"

"Half-sister."

"Don't quibble."

At home, Beryl got out of the car. When she turned to close the door, she noticed a damp looking spot on the back seat. She opened the back door to pat it, assuring herself it was probably a shadow, but no. The seat was damp. There was a small puddle on the floor mat too. An almost electrical spike of fear shook her from the inside out, she felt a bit of a chill. She took a few deep breaths, to shake it off, but that brought the scents of aftershave and stale cigarette smoke. She backed away shaking her head. Her heart was racing, and her hands shook so she almost dropped her phone. "No, no, no. Come on, be rational Beryl. Maybe there is a weakness in one of the window seals that the car wash breached. Take a deep breath and start a list for the dealer."

Hec was in the kitchen when she entered. It seemed overly bright to her. She squinted and blinked a little.

"Hey Hec, where's Abb?" she hoped he wouldn't detect the quaver in her voice.

"Fed and in bed Beryl."

"Not our Abby? It's only...."

"It's 9:45 Beryl. Abb and I've had dinner. Your plate's in the warming drawer. Glass of wine?"

Beryl checked her watch, the clock on the oven.

"Hec, I'm so sorry I didn't call. I was down in my zone on that new design." She was ashamed at how easily the lie came.

Hec shrugged, turned toward the wine glasses and asked again, "Glass of wine?"

"Uh huh, thanks."

During the drive in to work the next day Beryl was running a bit late but managed 15 minutes of the next episode. That night, a filthy, relentlessly wet night, she picked up where she had left off...

A woman's voice, "But, you don't know me."

"I don't need to know you." It was Dill.

"What have I done to you?"

"Me? Not a thing, doll. As far as I know you are a perfectly swell dame—though outta my league. Seems like a waste."

"Look can't you put that thing away? It might go off."

"It will go off darlin'."

"Why, why?"

"Better ask Delilo."

"Raimy?" a little snort and bright chuckle of relief, "Some kind of joke huh? OK buster, what's the hook?"

"No hook." Gun blast.

Beryl jumped. It surprised her how loud it seemed. She heard echoes of a muffled sound, a female "umph" and the rustle of someone slumping, only it didn't come from the speakers. The smell of cordite wafted from the back seat, then the sound of a wood match and the acrid smell of tobacco. She checked her rear-view mirror. There was an ember and a column of smoke. She swerved onto the shoulder, hitting the brakes, eyes snapping forward. She felt and heard that deep drone, like throat singing she experienced with her panic attacks. One side of her neck and jaw tightened, she could hear her own heart pounding, she struggled to force herself to breathe. She forced her eyes up.

She felt herself talking but didn't quite believe it. She didn't recognize her own voice.

"Say, put that out mister and don't toss it out the window either."

She felt something cold against her neck, she assumed it was a gun. Her hair lifted. Someone blew on her ear. Her hair dropped back down. She shivered, felt the cold sweat of fear in her armpits, yet her palms were relaxed on the wheel.

"Anyone ever tell you that you have a lovely neck?" She started to nod and tried a furtive glance in the rear-view mirror. "And don't get any ideas, get rolling again and keep those green eyes on the road and we'll all be pals, Irish."

"How far we going?"

"Not as far as I'd like."

Her voice sounded more familiar to her now, "My husband and daughter. They'll be worried."

"I'm sure they will darlin' but by the time they get around to doing anything about it, you'll be on your sweet way home, no harm done. But you sure you wouldn't consider forgetting that family right now and coming home with me, Irish? No? Too bad. I'm a sucker for red hair, green eyes, and those freckles. Take this turnoff down Five Mile Road. Wanna guess how far Five Mile Road goes?" he chuckled.

Beryl slowed and veered right, slowed some more as the roughness of the road surprised her. Her teeth were chattering but she didn't feel cold. Her hands were now shaking. Her insides were doing flip flops—

forget butterflies—she felt like some alien was about to emerge through her abdomen.

"OK, check your odometer, in 3 miles you'll see a turnout on the left. Use it for a U-turn but stop before you get back on the road. Watch the edge, it's steep."

She did as she was told. When stopped, she tried to get a look in the rear-view mirror.

"Careful now." She felt the cold barrel of the gun at the back of her neck again. She closed her eyes, wished she was practiced at prayer. "Hey." The gun tapped against her temple gently. "You better try breathing. Just keep your eyes forward and your hands on the wheel."

She heard the rear door open, some sliding, a thud. The car shifted with a weight change, shifted again. Whoever was in back slid across to the passenger side. Footsteps on gravel and something heavy being dragged, then nothing but the wind outside the open door. Footsteps headed back to the car. Another weight shift, the rear door closed. She heard heavier breathing.

"Dame didn't look to weigh that much. I guess death is like the camera, puts on the pounds. OK, you can head home. I'll tell you where to drop me and remember, eyes straight ahead, in fact, let's see you cock that rearview mirror to the side. Thatta girl."

"Who are you? What are you?"

"Eidolon." The voice, bored, carried a "no more questions" finality.

Eidolon. It rang a faint bell. Where had she heard that before? She heard a voice saying it, a different voice, not the voice from the back seat. Professor Dorelle, yes Ancient Greek Lit. Homer, Euripides Helen of Troy, Trojan Horse, all that. A shade, a spirit-image of someone dead or alive. She felt a chill. It was all she could do not to look back.

"OK." The voice from the back made her jump. "Know where the Greyhound station is?"

Beryl nodded.

"Drop me there."

Back home Beryl pulled silently into the garage. She sat staring. The door from the house to the garage burst open.

"Beryl, what the hell? I was worried sick. Abb too. I looked for your phone. What were you doing way out on Five Mile Road? Listen to me, like a fishwife. Come here you." Hec pulled her to him and squeezed. Rubbed his nose in her hair, sniffed deliberately a few times then pushed her back to look her in the eye. Did you start smoking?"

Beryl shook her head; her lips were quivering. Hec figured she was cold and led her into the house.

"Here, go put on your flannel lined jeans and a big sweater, I'll flip the basking machine on—you can eat near the fire. I kept your dinner warm—again—had to feed Abby. She's in bed but I'm sure she's not asleep. Better go assure her. She's still a little girl in a lotta ways you know."

"OK Hec. I'll wash my hair before I eat." Her voice low and rather monotone. She paused without looking around said, "I'm not smoking Hec. You know me better than that. I had to meet someone after work, chain smoker." Another lie.

She tried to use the shower to come 'round. "Buck up girl. Something has just triggered your vivid imagination in a powerful way. Remember the make-believe murder mysteries you used to solve as a kid while all your friends were playing with dolls? Creepy dolls." She shuddered and grinned at the same time. "I'm talking out loud to myself. If it happens again, I'll go see a trick cyclist."

She knew the water and steam in the shower was hot, still she shivered deep down. Finally gave up trying to stop shaking. Grabbed her big towel, then climbed into her hooded Turkish towel robe.

Beryl went directly to work the next morning, no scenic route, no *Noir In the 21ˢᵗ Century*. She tuned to a favorite internet radio station. An eclectic university campus non-profit.

"Daaa-ad?"

"Yes Aaaaaa-Abb."

"D'ya think you could take me shopping after school today? For a-a d-dress or something?"

"Ah, you want to dress up for mom's award dinner? A dress Abb? You? Really?"

"Don't make fun dad, yes, I-I d-do, I think it's im-important."

He felt bad, teasing her. He should have known how hard it was for her to ask. Her normally well-controlled stutter had re-surfaced. "Sure sweetie," he put one arm around her shoulder and squeezed. I'll cancel office hours with my students today. Meet you at the car after final bell?"

"Yip!" She launched herself at her dad and wrapped her arms around his neck and her legs around his legs—used to be hips. Hec marveled at how quickly he went from having a little girl to a long tall beauty.

"Want to go over to Anya's for a hair trim and a blow out too?"

"You're th-the b-best dad ever." She squeezed then hopped down giving him a peck on the cheek. "B-but she b-books up like crazy. What if she can't f-fit me in?"

"Remember, she's also Auntie Anya, I'm pretty sure we can work something out. In fact, it might be better—get your dress first, see her after the salon closes. She might want to check out your dress before styling your hair."

On the way home Beryl dismissed her reluctance to continue the podcast. The night was cold and windy, a freezing hard rain, with intermittent hail. She turned right, to the proverbial dark side of town and beyond, not left toward home. She checked her clock and figured she still had time to listen to one episode, get home and ready for her team's big gala that night. She'd arrive fashionably late, she grinned— it was almost expected of her now. She resumed the podcast. She felt she'd lost her place somehow. There was the sound of hard rain and wind being thrown against the windows. At a stop, the rear driver side door opened. A gloved hand covered her side mirror, the car shifted as someone got in…aftershave…the door closed, the light turned green. Beryl sat frozen.

Brenda put on her white gloves and polished Beryl's award. She admired it from several angles trying to decide which direction it should be facing for the unveiling. Settling on something she liked, she draped a plush deep blue velvet cloth over it. Brenda was proud to be on Beryl's team. This was the highest award their company offered, and it was rare. This was a design award, awarded by designers.

"Oh Brenda, Mr. Halliday wants to be sure Beryl has no inkling she's getting this tonight."

"Not as far as I can tell, Lucas, and I never thought of her having much of a poker face."

"…and she will make it tonight?"

"She won't be on time, but yes. I'm certain she'll be here."

"OK, we're doing the presentation between dinner and dessert service. She should be here by then." Lucas looked around the banquet room. "Looks good." He nodded, "Well, the band has arrived, sound system is a go, I'll just go peek in at catering."

"Don't attract attention now Irish. We're this close."

"Close? Close to what?"

"You tell me, doll, you tell me. I've got 'em bound and gagged just like you wanted. What's next?"

Beryl chilled from the inside out, her heart raced, her head felt like it would implode. "Who? What do you mean "like I wanted"?"

"We arranged it this morning. Don't you remember? Your kid and that husband of yours…"

"What do you mean? This isn't happening Beryl. Pull over, deep breaths, turn around drive straight home…"

"Hey, Irish, I thought you said it was you and me from here on out…"straight down the line" you said…anyway, rigged it so his car broke down on their way in to school…funny him teaching in the same school she attends. Along comes me, a good Samaritan, to give 'em a lift, right? It was real smooth. Your kid, she's sharp…had to move and talk fast to stay ahead of her. She knew my "shortcut" wouldn't work, had to pull off sooner than I wanted. Still, got 'em bagged and gagged. Introduced 'em to my dear wife. They can just go hungry together, most likely they'll die of exposure first."

Beryl went from chilled to flushed, she wanted to fling off all her clothes as she felt them tightening around her and such burning heat. "You're not real." Her voice cracked.

"Hurts to the quick, Irish. I feel real enough, that kiss last night was real enough."

"You yourself said 'Eidolon'. No, no, no, Beryl. Don't make him more real by talking to him. Turn off the podcast. Sing something. Sing something. Music heals me. *Rabbit of Seville* come on. She was pulling off the road, couldn't even come up with a tune, her hands were shaking, her whole body was shaking, tears dropped from her chin onto her chest she could hear her heart pounding, "Hec oh Hec what have I done, Abby, my baby you're OK, this isn't real."

She felt a warm hand pull her hair back behind her right ear, a caress lingered on her neck just below the ear, the familiar scent of aftershave, she felt her shoulders relax, her hands released the wheel. She leaned into the caress, took in a deep breath, she relaxed, and a smile spread across her face. Her head pressed into the warm hand, she rubbed her own cheek in his palm, then reached across and put her left hand over the back of his, kissed the palm. She rubbed a stubbled cheek with the back of her right hand. "Ah Dill, Dill." She felt herself talking. Heard herself, but her voice sounded sultry, husky, like a smoker's voice. "Gimme a drag, huh?"

Dill pulled the cigarette out of his mouth, turned it around and slid it between her lips at the side of her mouth. She took a deep drag, blew upward, a long spiral of smoke smashed against the headliner of the Leaf and spread out like a thunderhead. "You sure no one will find them?"

"Sure I'm sure doll, but you decide. They can starve in each other's company for all I care."

"We could get some cash for 'em...Dill, our money won't hold out forever...I bet Delilo isn't as hard-hearted about his half-sister as he makes out. Hec's family is filthy rich and they adore that granddaughter of theirs." She pulled out onto the highway.

"Isn't that a bit risky? You know, they might have a harder time pinning it on us if we all just disappear. Blackmail doll…I dunno."

"Blackmail beats murder. We go for the payoff, then disappear. Never to be heard from again. You and me, Dill, straight down the line."

The annual dinner carried on as these things do. Brenda, Lucas, and particularly Mr. Halliday kept a watch, at one moment on the door, at one moment on their watches, at one moment on the lovely sculpted award hidden under the cloth, at one moment on the three empty chairs where Beryl, her husband Hector, and daughter Abby were to be seated. The empty seats, the unused place setting were an irritation to Mr. Halliday. Beryl was often late, but this, this was rudeness, the annual gala. Of course, she didn't know about her award so she can't be blamed for snubbing it. The surprise was that Hector hadn't managed to get her there and he knew about this award. He always managed somehow to deliver Beryl at least "fashionably late."

Finally, the plates were cleared the speeches had begun.

Lucas bent down to whisper, "Mr. Halliday, Brenda and I have both called Beryl's and Hector's cell phones multiple times. We get no answer. I'm a little worried. I hope they haven't had an accident or something. This really is not like them." Lucas was, in fact, considering calling the police or local hospitals.

Brenda squatted down to add, "Mr. Halliday, if they don't arrive, I suggest you unveil her award anyway. The art department put so much into it, it is a lovely design in and of itself. You can make a joke about her tardiness. It's practically a signature for her…"

Dan Halliday, nodded, "Fine, fine." He made a whisking motion as though batting at a gnat to dismiss Brenda and Lucas. He could not disguise his irritation.

"Slow down, doll. Get us killed, you'll get them killed too…that long slow death you're trying to avoid. Though I hear that hypothermia can be pleasant after a while, after the first phases of cold they feel warm, even flushed, they start taking off their clothes and even try to burrow into a small dark space…"

Beryl pulled into an access road for a campground closed for the winter.

"I'm a city boy born and bred doll, what are we doing here?"

"Don't get cute, we gotta make a plan, I mean, how do we ask for the money? How do we arrange the pickup?"

"We don't have time for cut-out letter ransom notes. Phone calls?…too easy to trace."

"Unless…How about we use a burner phone even two or three? Make the calls from them. Have the money transferred via phone into, I dunno…Your wife's account is too obvious. Can't use Hec's either." Beryl started to tap her nails on the steering wheel.

"Biegler."

"Biegler?"

"Delilo's mouthpiece. He might do me a favor…for a cut."

"Why'd he help you burn Delilo?"

"Honor among thieves doll? Really?"

Beryl shrugged her shoulders.

"I bet I can get a nice little packet from Biegler. Burner phones, credit card account in some name or other ready and waiting, IDs, offshore bank account. We could get outta the country, and still get the money. Delilo will be quick. He'll also be ready to retaliate. What about your in-laws?"

"They'll need time to access their accounts I guess, I dunno how their money is locked up, bonds, stocks, bank. Probably need a day. So…you know how to contact Biegler?"

"Know where he lives. Head back to town. Just before city limits, take Majestic toward the lakes. Slow down, you're not driving a race car you know."

Beryl grinned, feeling she had the upper hand, "You're not scared are ya Dill? I just love the twisties although you're right, this isn't the car to do this road justice." Just then she hit some black ice, her Leaf spun and slid. The air bags didn't go off for some reason, her head hit the steering wheel hard. When she came to, she felt blood on the side of her forehead, grabbed a tissue. There was blood on the passenger window which she couldn't figure out. She didn't recognize the road she was on or her direction. The freezing rain didn't help. Thoroughly disoriented she shook her head to try to clear it, then grabbed her phone to pull up directions for home. The shoulder was only slightly canted, and it was easy for her to get turned around and back on the road.

She smelled cigarette smoke and aftershave. It puzzled her. The rain had completely given way to hail that was bouncing off her hood like ping pong balls. As she entered known streets and landmarks, she saw Hec's car on the side of the road. She smiled; he was out looking for her. She pulled up behind him and jumped out into the hail. As she got up to the driver door, she saw no one inside. She felt the hood of the car, cold. She felt a deep chill, heard the voice from the podcast "Still, got 'em bagged and gagged. Introduced 'em to my dear wife. They can just go hungry together, most likely they'll die of exposure first."

Cape Cod Resolve

Muriel, still in her dinner gown and stiletto pumps, hadn't gone to bed. Had he seen her? She was certain he had, so the real fear was, did he recognize her? Something had sparked in his shark eyes. His glance lingered through that spark. A question mark. So brief it could barely qualify as a glance. Ah, but Larson was too canny to let it slip into a look, let alone a stare. Too cunning to let on he recognized her. Shark eyes. Most of the time not even cruel, just empty. That's what made them chilling. There was simply no emotion, no humanity. Just some deep evolutionary throwback to pure survival instinct in a rough world. Did he recognize her? Follow her? Was he out there? She shivered. This chill, she knew, was not the morning. "Morning..." she whispered, stiff and surprised. Her awareness spread to her tight shoulders; arms stiff from supporting her upper body. Her hands frozen in their grip on the edges of the small round table tucked in the bay of the window.

Her palms and fingers tightened; the scars hummed like live wires. "Come on Muir, he can't have followed you—ME! He can't have followed ME." That inner critic was one of the warning signs her therapist told her to stay alert for, to keep in check. "You", the accusatory pointing finger of self-blame. She struggled with it ever since. She winced as she pushed herself upright with her hands. She stared at the surface of the table as the imprinted ghosts of her palms receded and disappeared from the polished maple. "Let's get you some of Dr. Trackman's magic balm. FUCK! Me, me, me, I, I, I, fuck, fuck, fuck! OK stop! Muir, stop. Deep breath..." She slipped off her ochre, open-toe pumps. She could still easily do an all-nighter in her four-inch stiletto heels, she allowed a grin. She savored the plush of the Kashmir rug with her feet, curled her toes into as if to grip the pile. Another deep breath and she padded down the hall to her vanity.

It hurt just to open the jar, yet she insisted. It was important to her that she do as much as she could, including being meticulous about maintaining orderliness. All jars, tubes, and bottles were closed and in their place. Dr. Trackman's prescription salve, which she thought of as her "magic balm", contained multiple components including a fast-acting topical analgesic along with slower acting components that had helped reduce the worst of the scarring and its side effects. It also helped her maintain a certain amount of flexibility. Dr. Trackman's "magic balm" was specially prepared by a compounding pharmacist and rivaled her finest cosmetics in cost, but it had also prevented her hands from turning into permanently curled and near-useless talons. In fact, as long as her palms and fingers were face down, and you didn't look too closely around the edges, she still had rather pretty hands. Muriel turned the scars away and allowed herself a moment to admire her long fingers. She collected a dollop of the balm and began to rub it in to her palms and fingers. Her shoulders relaxed then, slowly; her palms eased.

"Oh Effy! If only you hadn't left The Cape today." It was all Effy. Effy who had a masseuse's touch when she applied the balm on Muriel's hands. Effy, who as far as Muriel knew, was the only person on The Cape to know that Muriel was a matryoshka for Charlotte. Effy, who felled Larson with a shot to the back of the knee. Effy who then charged in without hesitation and coshed him on the back of the head with the butt of the little pistol she carried in her clutch. Effy who wrapped Charlotte's hands tightly in her best white Turkish towels. Effy who, even as the towels seemed to dye themselves crimson, steadied Charlotte and got her down to her 1937 LaSalle Touring Sedan. Effy who drove across Brooklyn Bridge to Dr. Trackman's brownstone on the edge of the Heights and woke him up. Effy who wiped Charlotte's forehead with a damp cloth and whispered "Ssh Ssshhh Ssh. You're alive baby, ok?" over her semi-conscious friend as the doctor cleaned and examined her hands prior to whatever restorative surgery he could do. Effy who, she later learned, asked the question "Doc, will she be able to play again?" Effy who steeled herself to a tough road ahead with her friend when she saw Dr. Trackman's eyes look down, his lips tighten, and his pained single sharp shake of his head. Effy who heard his sharp outbreath and saw him look over the top of his horn-rimmed glasses and heard his whispered "Only with a miracle, Eff. Only with a miracle."

"MREOOOOW! Prrrrrrrrrrrt, prrrrrrrrrrrt, mreoooow."

"Ruffian! Where have you been my big boy?"

"PRRRT!" replied the tortoiseshell and white Maine coon. His split ear in constant tremor, the scar on his cheek, looked like a chin tuck gone awry and sent his whiskers on the left side out in all directions like a cartoon blast. He stood with one big front paw on her left foot, rubbed her calf left and right like a European greeting, then banged her calf full on with his forehead. His loud purr like timpani in the hands of a genius.

"You don't want this stuff in your fur. Let me put on my gloves." Ruffian blinked in understanding and assent. She closed the lid to the balm, replaced the jar in its spot, and slipped on cotton gloves. Muriel bent down and scooped up fifteen pounds of cat, almost all muscle. They rubbed foreheads and she lingered a kiss between his ears, feeling the constant whisper tap of his ear tremor. Her forearm could feel the gentle press of claws as one big front paw flexed and released.

She carried Ruffian out front to the bay window, scanning the dawn, scanning the horizon. Nothing but the morning birds and distant susurration of the sea. The pitch-pine and oak forest on her left was a problem. But no...Larson wouldn't be out there. He was strictly city. He'd always had an aversion to anything green, anything he couldn't control. Still holding Ruffian, she turned to her phonograph. The turntable was still spinning, the needle playing "snick, snick, snick" against in the run-out groove of the record. She freed one hand to lift the arm and move the needle to the outer ring of the vinyl. A slight crackle, then the dynamic, tender, incongruously dissonant chords wordlessly crooned,

"Ruby, My Dear." It was almost as if the chords were the melody and the notes were the anchor. Thelonious Monk, turning tonal theory on its head, she hummed and smiled as she sat down in the darkest corner of the room opposite the window. Ruffian still allowed her to hold him. He always knew when something was amiss with his girl. He waited, soft and heavy in her grasp. Her gloved fingers, subconsciously played along, picking out the characteristically Monk chords and distinct melody in Ruffian's double-coated fur. The song ended, again the needle hung in the run-out grove, "snick snick snick".

"He's here." Muriel whispered in Ruffian's soft warm neck.

It was a beautiful afternoon. Effy pulled up the circle drive, surprised Muriel and Ruffian weren't sitting on the veranda having their afternoon tea, and tuna water with Muriel reading out loud and Ruffian listening and cleaning himself next to her in their big wicker swing chair.

She hopped out of the car, firmly pushed the car door shut. Reaching in through the open back window she grabbed a box wrapped with string off the back seat.

"Muir!" No answer. "Ruffian! Kittykittykitty!" No cat trotted out to greet her, tail high and bouncing.

"Muriel?" her shoes seemed to whisper as she came up the steps, she felt a wave of uncertainty and wished, briefly, she still carried her "little popgun" as she called it. Earl made her learn how to use it and carry it. She never really liked having it except for that one night—the only time she ever used it. The house was locked up tight, she had to dig in her clutch for her key. She could feel her breath shallow and short as she slowly tried to open the screen door without a sound and slip her key in the lock. She opened the door to shadow now made starker by the contrast of the parallelogram of sun as it shone through the bay to her left. There was a delay as her eyes adjusted from bright sun to indoor dim. Effy reached her arm behind her and slowly set the box down on the catchall table by the door. She kicked one foot out behind her to catch the screen door before it screaked and banged shut.

"Prrrt?"

"Oh Ruffian!" She looked in the direction of the sound and there in the darkest corner of the room, curled in the fan-backed swivel club chair sat Muriel, Ruffian in her lap and now sitting up alert and facing Effy. Muriel's half-closed eyes that didn't look up at Effy made the back of her spine tingle.

"Muir? Muriel honey?" No reaction. She slipped off her sling backs and padded over to the chair. She scratched Ruffian on the chin, rubbed his forehead and gently put her other hand on Muriel's shoulder. She bent down close to Muriel's ear, "Charlotte?" she whispered.

Muriel raised bloodshot eyes to Effy. "He's here. I saw him at the the Club Eff."

Effy slowly squatted down to sit at Muriel's feet. She reached out and put her hand on them. They were cold as ice, she covered them with both hands, rubbed them. Thoughts and questions were gathering, but Muriel wasn't up to them now. Effy slowly collected herself.

"OK honey, OK. Does he know you are here?"

"I, I can't know that...I don't think so, but he did see me, our eyes met, he oh he..."

"OK Sshhh. Let's get you warmed up, fed, and changed." She rubbed Ruffian's head and rubbed his injured ear between index finger and thumb. She was the only one allowed to touch that ear. "You good big guard cat. Let's get you some nice tuna."

"Prrrt bbbrrrrOW!"

"Muriel dear?" No response. Effy leaned in close to Muriel, one hand on each shoulder and gave a consoling gentle grip, "Muriel, you cannot be Charlotte, you know. You know that, don't you? Don't you?"

Muriel nodded slowly.

"OK, good," she patted Muriel's left shoulder and straightened up. "I'm going to rustle up something for you and get Ruffian's tuna. I'll be right back."

Effy went down the hall to fill the bath and set out towels and robe. While the tub filled, she went to the kitchen and opened the promised tuna for Ruffian and started preparation for tea and toast. She grabbed a hard-boiled egg out of the refrigerator and checked the avocados.

She could hear "Ruby My Dear" from down the hall and knew Muriel was standing up, she padded into the living room to find Muriel swaying to the music, humming quietly while staring out the bay window.

"Come on Muir," Effy gently took Muriel's elbow, "your bath is almost ready." She escorted Muriel down the hall to the tub, then returned to the kitchen.

Effy sat a tray with sliced egg and avocado on toast on a little bench within reach of the tub. Her tea was in Muriel's big French mug—almost a bowl really. The hot bubble bath was already reviving Muriel. When Effy next checked on her, the haunted look had faded. Muriel now looked almost undaunted. Muriel not Charlotte. The egg and avocado on toast had been consumed by both Muriel and Ruffian. The big cat was perched in perfect balance on the rim of the tub next to the tray. A telltale piece of egg yolk lingered at the side of his mouth while he avidly licked up the remaining butter from the saucer. Muriel was holding the tea in both hands, her chin rested on the rim, eyes closed, breaths deep and slow. Effy slipped away to leave them to their privacy. She found herself standing at the bay window, the window where Muriel had stood watch most of the night. It was a good window. Usually used for viewing their lovely surroundings, and letting in the amazing Cape light, but also good for ruminating and, apparently last night, for watchfulness.

"How could she have seen him? Can he be alive?" Effy knew the gunshot wound to the knee had not hit anything serious enough to cause more than pain, a scar, and a possible limp. Still, she always thought she'd accidentally killed him with the blow to the head. Once Dr. Trackman had prepared Charlotte and himself for surgery, he told Effy the procedure alone would take hours. The sedative would take time to wear off so there was nothing for her to do. He offered her a cot to sleep on. She declined. She had unfinished business. Earl would help her. She thanked the doctor, kissed Charlotte on the forehead and drove off.

She found Earl at the usual club with the usual group of young toughs. She caught his eye and hooked her head in a meet me outside gesture. Earl stood up, he seemed about three times as big as any man in the room. As he weaved through the crowd for the door, one could see he wasn't bound up or clumsy. He had a dancer's way of moving with the body of a heavyweight. He had a vacuous look, like there was nobody home. This is what made him so dangerous, because there was most definitely somebody home and he was intelligent. Effy's dad had gotten Earl out of a jam and he'd floated around Effy and her little brother ever since, watching and waiting for a day when they needed him. He had also fallen in love with Effy, but never let on—or so he thought. Effy felt it was more convenient for him to believe she was clueless about it. Better all round.

"Earl, I need your help."

He just nodded, followed her to the car and got in. They drove in silence and pulled into the garage below the hotel, she found a parking spot in an area of the garage where the lights had gone out. She felt like a child standing shoulder to elbow with him in the elevator, she also felt comforted. As soon as they got in the apartment, he saw Larson on his stomach, face turned away from view, his knife still in one fist the bloodied blade stark against the cream plush of the rug. Earl turned and put out an arm to stop Effy from getting any closer.

He held out his right hand and bounced it in a quick gesture curling his fingers in. She handed him the car key. He pulled out a wad of cash and handed it to her, "Taxi." She nodded. He looked at the bloody knife blade. "Charlotte?"

"Her hands Earl, her hands..." A deep anger flashed in his green eyes, then a great sadness. He put his hand softly on her shoulder and with the light pressure of a dance partner steered her to the door. "Dr. Trackman?" She nodded, as she stepped out. She barely heard the door close. She heard her own steps in the carpeted hall. She heard the whirs and bells of the elevator. She still remembers those sounds. She knows nothing of what Earl did that night. The next time she saw their rooms, all was sparkling clean. She picked up the phone and gave notice that she and Charlotte were moving out.

So yes, Larson could be alive...

She heard the tub draining, the rustling of towel and robe, then the bright sounds of empty china rattling as Muriel carried the tray back to the kitchen. She came out to the living room, started "Ruby My Dear" over on the turntable. Effy turned to her. Before she could speak, soft footsteps coming up the front porch stairs then crossing the porch gave them both a start, but Ruffian issued his "Prrrrrt mmreow!" of greeting and trotted towards the door. They relaxed a little but Effy still pushed Muriel into the shadow of the hall.

Before Effy could get to the front door, the screen door opened then Dusty's smoky voice muffled by the front door opening called out,

"Muir? Eff? Muir hon' it's," the "just me" was louder as she popped her head in the door. She brushed the sand off her feet and slipped in the room barefoot, tight turquoise pedal pushers, a man's shirt tied at her midriff, her blond hair so short it startled most people. A pair of beige Huarache-inspired wedge sandals dangled from the first two fingers of her left hand; acrylic stains outlined her fingernails. Muriel and Effy stepped forward relieved and they all bussed each other cheek to cheek.

"I just wanted to stop by Muir," she switched her attention to Effy, "Glad you're back Eff. You know we were having a great time at the club last night. Frank and Muir were out on the dance floor one minute, the next she just stopped cold, headed back to our table and asked to leave. She said she could take a taxi, but the way she looked, huh uh. We brought her back. We offered to come in, but she insisted she'd be OK. Had to come by, sorry it's so late...we slept...well." She looked down, "Yes my big boy. Let Dusty give you a big hug." Ruffian was standing with front paws on her thighs big bottlebrush tail floating upward and swaying like grasses in a breeze. She reached under his forearms, and picked him up, kissed his nose, butted him forehead to forehead and hugged him to her.

"Soooo?" she shrugged, looking a question mark from Muriel to Effy and back.

Muriel answered "I think I was just exhausted, that's all. I'm fine Dusty, would you like some tea? Coffee? Something a bit stronger?"

"No no" bending to put Ruffian down, "I want to get back, I got some new ideas for my painting on the walk over...I've been stuck, want to get back before I lose the image... Frank and I are thinking of going back to the club tonight. Why don't you two join us? Dinner? 7 o'clock cocktails? We'll pick you up. Ciao!" and without waiting for an answer and with a screak-bang of the screen door she was off padding through the sand, her back still to them, her sandals waggling at them suspended from her waving hand.

"Muriel, you sure?"

"Effy, I've got to know. I must know if he's still around. I must know if it was even really him. Maybe it was just some guy unfortunate enough to resemble him just enough and my anxiety brought back the nightmare. I've gotta face life Eff."

"If it was him, and he's still in town? If he saw you? Sees you? What then?"

"I'll be careful that he doesn't get a good look Eff. I'm not sure his imagination is that good anyway. Remember he bought my act from Lenny. He only knew me like Lenny had me made up for the stage, you know. Dyed black hair pale make-up hiding my freckles...had some crazy notion that the look mirrored the ebony and ivory. That it added something for the folks listening. Larson thought it was working so didn't make a change. I don't think he had a clue I was a redhead." Effy gave her a rakish look with a head tilt, one eyebrow raised. Muriel blushed. "Shit Eff, everything was waxed. I dressed in the gowns he bought me, he was only around when he took me to the club to play, and well, after...after those nights..." she shivered, "...until he found out about the recording contract...I never shoulda told him Eff..." her voice trailed off as did her gaze. She gathered herself.

"Effy! But Effy, you! What about you? What can we do? I mean, if it is him..."

"So my hair style is different, I could go to Marge and have her dye me up...no...no...somebody might comment within his hearing... I'll wear one of my hats..." She grinned and reached out and gripped Muriel's forearm briefly, excited as a little girl with a new toy, "Muir! My new little pillbox with a veil! I just bought it! You're gonna love it!" Animated she went to get the box she'd sat down next to the door when she had returned.

The billboard outside the club read "The Arresting Alice Faye Waring on the piano! New York's latest best kept secret here for three nights only! She croons. She plays. Classical, Jazz, Blues and she can Boogie Woogie too!" Muriel and Effy were both drawn to the print centered at the bottom "Courtesy of Larson-Loon Talent Promotions". They looked grimly at each other. Effy was about to offer they leave now when Muriel's shoulders set, back and down. Effy knew then Muriel was not ready to retreat. They followed Frank and Dusty in. Muriel spoke up first when the head waiter came over "George, not our usual tonight if you don't mind. Can we have a table at the back just for tonight? A little "inside" joke...something Frank said..." George smiled and winked and led them to a table for four under the overhang on the periphery of the room, nice and dark.

Cocktails on the way, there was activity up in the stage area. A spotlight lit up on a Bösendorfer. Lionel, the manager came out with a mic: "Ladies and gentlemen, thank you for coming tonight, we are proud to present for the first time on The Cape the lovely, the talented Miss Alice Faye!"

Polite applause, the sounds of cocktails and silverware on china, low conversation. A spot lit the side curtain which fluttered then through it emerged a dark-haired beauty in a semi-revealing deep navy velvet gown. She walked slowly as if concentrating on not falling out of her heels. She settled herself, straightening the gown at the seat, and revealing a long expanse of back, then she leaned into the mic, positioned so she could speak into it while looking at the audience. Then like flipping on a light switch she turned on the charm. The background noise all but ceased. She nodded a thanks and without a word started to play and sing: "You...ain't be-en bluuuuu...". She played a nice jazz and blues variety including "easy to dance to" nightclub favorites and then said, well, before I take a break, I believe the billboard promised some boogie woogie. I'm no Jay McShann, but here's a little "Vine Street Boogie" and I'll try not to mess it up too much. She launched into a pretty fair rendition, not too fast, not too slow a mistake many make with the boogie woogie rhythm.

After the set, Muriel had to force herself to patiently finish her meal and stay engaged in the conversation. She told herself she had plenty of time between sets, still, it was a challenge. She took her last bite of her Peekytoe Crab Cakes placed her fork at 3 o'clock, tines down on her plate and stood, stooping briefly to leave her napkin on the seat. "Excuse me." to the table, a longer look between her and Effy.

Muriel headed toward the "Ladies" until she was out of site then veered to the backstage rooms where she knew she'd find Alice Faye. The door was slightly ajar, she tapped it lightly, stepped in and quietly closed the door as Alice Faye turned, and frowned, "Do I know you?"

"No Alice Faye—you do use first and middle?"

Alice Faye nodded and affirmed sharply "Please." Her look, a little cold, mostly cautious, but not outright unwelcoming.

Muriel was undeterred "How long have you been with Larson?"

"Three months. What's it to ya?"

"Ah! So…the honeymoon is not over." Muriel said with a sadly sarcastic, knowing smile.

Alice Faye threw a hand down as though striking something "Hah! Say look, we're not even married, Larson is just my promoter, see?" She held out her left hand as though admiring a ring on her third finger and her tone softened "Although…little Alice Faye could use a bit of a faerie tale in her life. She turned toward a chair and nodded at its mate opposite. "Siddown, take a load off!" She kicked her dark blue velvet pumps off with a sigh of relief. "One of these days I'll convince him kitten heels can be elegant and sexy too. My poor feet, I swear!" She lifted the hem of her dark blue velvet gown up to her knees and crossed her left leg over her right knee and pulled her stockinged foot onto her lap. She immediately started to rub it. "Feel free." She gestured for Muriel to do the same.

Muriel grinned, shook her head "You know sometimes I think I must have been born in heels." She looked admiringly at her four-inch stilettos with the steel tap, her latest acquisition from Ferragamo. "I find them quite comfortable."

Alice Faye shook her head, then looked up suddenly "Say! You know my name, so whaddoeye call you?"

"Muriel, you may call me Muriel."

"OK, Muriel, so what? You here to request a shleppy song for your anniversary my next set or what? A tip? Rare praise at my prowess at the keyboard, you think the camera would love me and you want to take me to Hollywood? What?"

Muriel demurely mouthed a "no" she shook her head slowly and collected herself. "No. Well, maybe a tip after a fashion, yes, a tip. It could land me in a jam if you say anything to…to him." She made a backward nod with her head."

Alice Faye paused her foot rub to look up at Muriel with a hard look. "Well, so no one owns me, OK? And I don't owe you nuthin' but neither have I got reason to snitch on you. Hate snitches. Snitches took my dad away. Left mom and I in pretty sorry shape, too. So OK what gives?"

Muriel locked eyes with Alice Faye's snapping dark eyes. Summing her up. She clearly had a different background to Charlotte, because here now in this capacity she was Charlotte once again. None of Charlotte's privileges. Alice Faye shifted to switch legs and rub her right foot.

Charlotte watched her. With Alice Faye once again looking at her foot she saw a vulnerability. She thought, *Still, different as we are, I like her. I trust her. She's had it tough enough it seems.*

Resolved, without a word, Charlotte turned both hands over, palms up and extended them toward Alice Faye who was absorbed with her foot. The silence and shadow that moved into her periphery caught Alice Faye's eye and she looked up. She started with a sudden intake of breath through her open mouth. It caught in her throat, "UH!" Silence was not a realm of comfort for Alice Faye but, for a time, she uttered not a sound. She reached out with her own hands palms also facing up, flawless palms, long fingers void of angry red and white welts, void of a crisscross of scar tissue. Slowly she turned her palms face down as she quietly slid off the chair onto her knees. She scooted closer to Muriel and sat back on her heels. "May I?" She whispered to Muriel. At Muriel's nod Alice Faye gently rested her hands over Muriel's. A mascara-stained tear drew a clown line down Alice Faye's right cheek. She traced the length of Muriel's scarred fingers, so gently, a butterfly's touch. "Larson?"

Muriel nodded and their eyes locked by an unseen force, an electrical charge. Alice Faye gently turned Muriel's hands over and placed them on Muriel's knees. Then suddenly, she propelled herself off the floor, immediately pacing like a great angry cat in the zoo. "Son of a bitch! Son of a fucking bitch!" Her head was shaking as she paced, she was almost roaring. "Son of a...say!" Her voice dropped. "Say, he better not find you here, Muriel or whatever your name is. Don't worry about me now. 'Forewarned is forearmed' as they say." Still she paced. Muriel stood up, caught up with Alice Faye and put her hands lightly on her shoulders. Alice Faye turned to see her concerned face. "No, no. Don't worry about me." She turned to her mirror and wiped off the mascara track, took a deep breath and turned around with a big smile, her stage smile. Expertly, she snatched a cigarette off her dressing table and lit it, almost in a single fluid gesture. "See." She blew out the match sensuously, almost elegantly. Calmly her voice now void of accent "See? Yes, I can put on an act." Back to her own voice "I can put on an act alright, see? Matter of survival where I grew up. Now you gotta get outta here. I don't know you, see?" She gently pushed Muriel out the door, her last whispered words, "I got friends from that old neighborhood, see? And, thanks kid. That took real guts."

The door snicked shut.

Hester's World

In a perfect world. I live in a perfect world. It is my world. My reality. My version. When did I first get an inkling that it wasn't a real world? I pushed it away far away the idea was too frightening. If this is not real, what is and how do I find it? Where do I find it? How do I cope in it? Where do I fit in it? Am I a non-entity in it? Is it kind or cruel, funny or sad, safe or scary? Is it a void and I alone? Completely and utterly alone? Just me, no one else. Or is it crowded, so crowded I go unnoticed? People all around but no friends. But I have no friends now, ah but I do. Indeed, I do, perhaps they are figments of my imagination, but they are mine and they are friends. Is it a malady? I don't know if I want to be cured. I'm afraid of being alone, truly utterly alone in the world, or simply lonely and lost in a crowd.

I feel all folded over in the middle. Like a beer can that hasn't been successfully crunched flat, bent over forward, but one side, the backside sort of like a humpback. Wunderly. What a great name. Good first lines in *The Maltese Falcon*, John Huston used the exact lines of dialog in the beginning of the movie.

Quiet, here comes my own personal Psycho. She's lovely. Nefertiti eyes. I think she practices hypnotherapy on me. So I kind of go away. She learns things about me and hopes I remember them, but I don't. I try to pretend in order to please her. If every waking moment is a dream how can that be analyzed? How does that help? How did I get here? I don't remember. Maybe I invented this place. Pretty painted walls in an effort not to be white and sterile and hospital like. Just the same I hear locks and keys and keypads and card key beeps. Why so many different methods for so many different doors? I don't even know if I've met any of my fellow...what? Inmates is it? Are they? Are we? If I have met any of them, I wouldn't know if they are real or my own creations. No if you are thinking it stop right now, I don't think I'm some sort of a god. Rhapsody. I feel a rhapsody coming on, but I have no paper to pen the notes to. Who would perform it anyway? I'll never be discovered, especially not here.

Nefertiti just walked in, well no I didn't see nor hear her walk in. I just looked up and she was there in the chair she uses by the open window. My chair is just the other side of the window. We sit at angles, our knees near to each other. It is a small window. A gust just blew the gauze curtain across her face like a veil revealing only one lovely eye. She laughed as her long blue nails lifted the veil from her face, it retained a bit of dark red lipstick and brown face powder.

"Lovely day, where are your sunglasses? Shall we go outside?"

No, she never used the "How are we today?" line, but the "Shall we go outside?" was not really a question. It didn't feel like an order either, simply a quiet direction as if she knew what I would like to do. Or knew what would be good for me to like to do.

So, then we were in the garden, I don't recall the door being unlocked, the walk down the hall, the next door being unlocked, the back recreation hall and the patio door being unlocked. Not the walk down the path. Just here we were in the herb garden. With bees. We were in beekeepers' garb and tending to the racks of honey carefully. Quietly. We didn't speak to each other. Our eyes would meet when one of us would hold out a particularly lovely hive tray. It was like a ballet. A chorus of bees flew in and out of the hives. When we spoke, we whispered salutations and praise to the bees. I reached out my gloved hand and pet one with my little finger, so gently. The bee tolerated it, for a moment then buzzed away. We spent the morning among the bees. If I imagined this world, this was one of my best moments. Like Slartibartfast and the fjords. I looked down. We were barefoot. Everywhere else covered with protective beekeepers' garb except our feet. Mine pale from not having seen the sun in so long, Nefertiti's golden brown, darker on the top, I could just see inside the arch of her right foot, more gold than brown. My toenails bare and uneven. Nefertiti's were perfect, and blue like her fingernails. A bee would land on top of a foot then fly away, uninterested.

The world looked different from within the beekeeper uniform. The gauze over the eyes softened everything. The hum and buzz of the bees and in such proximity with so many I swear you could also hear the soft rush of their wings as though taken all together they created a soft breeze and susurration. I liked this world from within my beekeeper clothing. Maybe it wasn't necessary to have protection from the bees, but it offered me protection from the unfiltered world. The world where things were harsh and brash and sharp and glaring and loud and shrill.

Nefertiti and I worked side by side in silence she was not my therapist, she was my companion, but then maybe she was both they don't have to be mutually exclusive, do they? But did she feel I was a companion or was that one-sided and meant to be part of the therapy?

There was a shift like deep in the universe it seemed, scents of the herbs seemed almost louder than the bees. Nefertiti inserted the last honey tray into the end hive. She turned and scanned the entire horizon making a slow graceful dancelike 360-degree turn, her feet, the same size as mine, ten, seemed more graceful than my feet, they traced a pattern as she turned, just like a dancer. She took a deep breath and turned to me. Her focus was still far to the horizon, I was foreground noise, then she smiled as her focus fixed on my eyes. She put her right hand on my shoulder just a touch, then motioned toward the path and the building with her left, like ushering me into the presence of a great being.

Then I was in my room. Alone. But the scent of aloe and sage and desert lingered, I walked into the air where the scent was strongest, closed my eyes and breathed in until it dissipated. Then I felt lonely and turned to my wicker chair in the corner by the window. The sun had warmed the old faded cushions they'd been a vermillion print once upon a time. The chair and cushions formed my back perfectly. The wicker had a welcoming creak, "Hello Hester, relax, read, sleep, I'll hold you safe and warm."

I heard the locks of my door this time, but kept my eyes closed. I knew it would be Willem bringing me something hot to drink. I always supposed it was a vehicle for some medication, but I never could taste it. A nice green tea with ginger and something else a hint rosehip? Sometimes he left a flower on the saucer. I didn't smell one this time, rather mint yes, a sprig of mint and a sprig of parsley. As soon as I heard him leave, I opened my eyes to see if my guess was correct. Yes! I get small pleasures from these guessing games. I longed for Thursday. On Thursdays, Nickelodeon spent the afternoons with me. He would jump into my lap as soon as I was settled, sniff my tea, scan outside the window for prey, then curl up purring in my lap. I would pet him between sips of tea or turns of the page of a book. He had the smoothest fur I'd ever touched. Thursdays I smiled more than any other day, I slept better on Thursdays. I don't know what Nickelodeon does the rest of the week. I wish he were mine all mine. Or rather, I alone was his, we don't own cats.

Suddenly I realized I'd lost track of time, not time of day, but time of week. I didn't know how long I had to wait for Thursday. I stood up, spilling a little tea on the floor, I spread it around with my foot, dried my foot on my pants leg. I paced the room between the door and the window, I finally stopped at the window seeking some sign that would remind me what day it was. It seemed like forever since last Thursday. Have they stopped allowing Nickelodeon in to see me? NO! NO! They can't have. I won't eat. That's what, I'll show them. I gripped the window frame, my legs, I jiggered my legs bending one knee then locking it, the other leg the reverse. I must have missed the sound of the locks, but I felt something brush one leg, then the other. I stopped moving. I heard a loud purring. I was so relieved I bent down and picked Nickelodeon up and buried my face in the ruff of fur at his neck. I was still shaking I couldn't sit down, I rocked him. He allowed it momentarily, then I sat down, he sniffed what was left of my tea, chewed a little of my parsley and curled up in my lap.

I dreamt I was floating in warm water. All around me were surgeon fish, big friendly fish with brilliant blue and yellow markings. Smaller fish too of many varieties and colors including those pretty coffee brown fish. I looked down in the strip of sand between coral bands to see a magnificent snake eel moving along the sand in search of shrimp. Further along, I saw a moray, resting half out of his cave. I let myself be moved by the current, slow and calm. I could hear whales in the distance, then the hull of a sailboat passing.

"Hester! Hester! Time for dinner." It was Sundra. She let me eat in my room on Thursdays so the crowded loud cafeteria wouldn't wipe away all the good Nickelodeon's visit had done me.

"Hamburgers tonight I'm afraid." She said.

My eyes were still closed, I groaned but I didn't smell hamburger grease. I don't dislike all hamburgers, but I disliked these hamburgers.

She laughed, "Keep them closed. Can you guess what Les fixed special for you instead?"

I could sense that she was wafting something under my nose. It smelled clean and fresh, then I detected kalamata olives and feta cheese. I clapped and smiled, "Greek salad! Oh Les! Hug him for me would you Sundy? If its permitted and if it isn't do it anyway but don't get caught."

She laughed, plucked an olive off my salad and popped it in her mouth with a wink. I winked back. One of her thick soled shoes squeaked against the floor as she turned to go. She started to sing *Aquas de Marco* in the original Brazilian Portuguese. In English it translates to *Waters of March*. A favorite from Antonio Carlos Jobim.

She knew what calmed me down. She had the cool beautiful smooth voice required for that music. Lovely. As soon as I began to hum and smile, she left me alone with scents of Brazil, the beach, and the tune still in my head.

Nefertiti didn't come the next day. She sent me a bundle of eucalyptus with one red flower, a hibiscus, and a little drawing. A self-caricature of her in a small wooden sailboat. She held the tiller in one hand, the other waved and one long leg was hanging over the side with her foot dangling in the water. A water drop fell from her hair, her bandeau and wrap skirt, wild floral print looked wet. How she captured that I do not know.

I pasted it to a new page for my scrap book but taped the page to the wall opposite my chair so I could admire her drawing for a while before closing it in the book.

"Hes! Hester. Hes!" I started, uncrossed my legs and my bare foot stepped on the spine of the book I'd dropped when I fell asleep. I looked around and at first didn't see anyone.

"Hes, I came to take you for a walk since doc…your friend can't come today."

It was Sundra's voice. I followed the sound. It took me awhile to locate her in the room. She was camouflaged against the wall, her uniform blended with the paint.

"Yes, I know. Thank you Sundy." I headed to the door, dragging my fingers through my hair, some of it fell out and was wrapped around my fingers, I couldn't shake it off. "Let go! Let go of me!"

"Sh Sh Sh, Hes." Sundy started to hum something with a samba beat as she gently cleared the hair from my hands. "Where are your shoes?"

"Don't."

"You'll ruin your feet."

"Won't."

"How about your flip flops?"

I sat back down hard and crossed my arms. Said I was cold.

Sundra changed the tune sang more of a bossa nova in Portuguese. I wanted to walk on a sandy beach. She pulled something out of a bag she'd dropped just inside the door.

"Espadrilles?" She waved them, a bright orange with rope ankle ties.

I jumped up and clapped then skipped over to her, swiped them out of her hands blew her a kiss and bending my knee raised one foot behind to slip one on, then likewise other side. I squatted down to wrap and tie them, then danced around the room to her song.

We bossa novaed out the door. Sundra was Brazil, Jobim, Astrud Gilberto, Elis Regina.

Nefertiti was Olatunji African drums, Miles Davis, Bitches Brew.

Both brought their own type of music and sunshine into my world.

We strolled, Sundra continued to hum, we strolled, a dance, with our arms around each other's waists. We entered the aviary full of color, flora, feathers, songs that wove through Sundy's humming, she played with the bird song as we passed through. There were scents of honeysuckle, plumeria, gardenia, jasmine, ginger. Flapping. There was a lot of flapping. We each took a cup of diced mango from the feeding station. Birds landed on our arms to eat. They never weigh what I expect from their size.

We continue through the Aviary to the koi pond where we both squat down and pet the fish. A tone came from Sundy's wrist. I knew it was her timer and our stroll must come to an end.

Felicia is my real name. I know this, though I don't remember anything else about me. They don't know it. I told them my name was Hester. I don't want them to find anyone from my past. I don't know why. I don't remember how I got here. I woke up. That's all. At first, I thought I was in a hospital bed. Someone was bent over me asking my name. When I opened my eyes, he smiled at least his eyes smiled, he had a mask over his nose, mouth, chin. But he had nice eyes. Kind eyes. "I'm Dr. Fanshaw. We'll be getting you back on your feet." I'm not really sure if I meant to lie about my name. At first, I really wasn't sure of my name. Everything was fuzzy. After hearing the question, softly and kindly put to me I felt an obligation to answer and so I said Hester. Just that. Then he said, "That's fine Hester. Now, can you tell me your last name?" I couldn't. I nearly panicked, he must have seen it, he put his hand on my shoulder and the other hand over my hands and said, it was OK. It could wait. They are still waiting.

Truth is I really don't remember my last name. I guess one of these days I might come up with something. There is a man in an office I see. He has pictures on his desk. Him on a paddle board with a huge dog, tall, long legged. A woman on a paddle board with the same dog. She's pretty. He is the first person who talked to me in this place. I saw the two pictures right off and instead of returning his greeting of welcome and introduction I nodded at the photos and asked "But, where's the cat?"

He turned around and grabbed another photo off the cabinet behind him and set it down in front of me. The same woman, holding a leash attached to a harness attached to a big black and white cat with a fine square jaw. The cat is watching something in a pond. Looking back, I now recognize it as the koi pond right here on the grounds.

"He likes to watch, never tries to catch anything. Would you like to see your room now?"

On a recent visit to him I lied. It was to please him really.

"Please do sit down Hester. Speaking of which, you don't yet recall your last name do you Hester?"

I shrugged my shoulders and rolled my eyes up in an exaggerated pantomime of thinking. "Something that I think starts with an M maybe. Mi- Mi-. Not Mississippi, not like a state."

"Good. Keep sounding it out Hester, like a game. How many words or names can you think of that start with that sound?"

I liked him. He seemed kind, patient. I decided to make a show of trying.

"Mit? Middle? Mine, Mite, Mike, Mire, Mile, Mile? Miles…Miles Mile zone? Miles…Milestone? Maybe Milestone? Is that a good name?"

"It is a good name Hester, but is it your name?"

"I, I think so. Maybe?"

"That's fine. That's a good start. Live with it awhile. We'll put it down in pencil so we can change it if you think it isn't really your name."

I nodded. He stood up and put his hand out for me. I stood up my elbow found his outstretched hand and he walked me to the door. That's when I met Sundra and Jake. The doctor shook his head at Jake, who looked like a bouncer, a fair and kind bouncer. He was probably there in case someone might be resistant or try to escape or something. Jake was a good guy. I got to know him better as he sometimes took me outside up into the hills that bordered the grounds. I could really breathe up there I could tell the hills, the view, the rigorous walk up the trail impacted him in the same way. He taught me sign language. American and his own from the Navajo nation. I used to know a little ASL, I could only remember rudimentary things, some of the alphabet. We got by, he was a pretty good lip reader and laughed at my makeshift signs and liked my little sketches in the dirt. I had found a stick I particularly liked to use to draw and write for him on the trail. We always left it at the trailhead up in the crotch of a tree that looked like a dancing man with a funny haircut.

Our silences came easy on those walks. People were always bringing me shoes. It started though with Jake, he brought me some over the ankle trail shoes and hiking socks. Did they measure my foot when I was unconscious? They sure fit like a glove even down to the high arch support and I loved them. Deep rich brown with red laces.

There he is now. He has a special cadence to punching the code into a keypad. One day I'll recall what song it reminds me of.

I smiled and pointed at my eye with my index finger then patted my chest in a rolling motion with fingers pointed to him.

Jake smiled at my clumsy attempt to tell him I was happy to see him.

He patted his hiking boots and pantomimed walking up something with his fingers. I nodded and smiled and grabbed my boots from my little shoe shelf tucked under my bed.

He never sat down in my room. I don't know if it had to do with his customs or if he was afraid he'd crush the wicker chairs. He never seemed impatient or uncomfortable. He was a man wholly himself. Strong. Kind. He was the one they'd send to me when I was having a panic attack. He would sing in his true language, his Navajo tongue. It was like warm open space, a cathedral, a warming breeze, a deep breath, sunshine. I wanted to learn it. He smiled kindly as he shook his head and pressed one big brown hand to his heart. A tree, a mountain, fresh air, warmth.

He wrote his real name for me one day in the dirt. Gáagii. A crow happened to land at the very top of a nearby tree. Gáagii pointed at the bird, then he pointed at his name written in the dirt, then he nodded and pointed at his chest. I asked Sundra if she could find out how to pronounce it for me. The G is a hard g like in gate. It rhymes with groggy soggy smoggy, but its meaning is far more beautiful than those words. She also found out it could be raven or crow. I wondered how they got "Jake" out of that. I wondered what was wrong with learning his real name. I have always loved ravens, crows, rooks. They are so smart and make good friends. Before I came here, I remember bad bad days, a crow would appear and make me smile. I found them reassuring. It was a good name.

One sunny afternoon Gáagii came in and found me curled up on the floor asleep in a strip of sun. He woke me gently and helped me up so we could take our walk. The next day after keeping bees with Nefertiti I returned to my room and found a beautiful Navajo rug laid out in that same strip of sun. I curled up on it, it was warm and had desert scents of sagebrush and creosote bush. I felt a smile on my face as I drifted off to sleep.

RGB 255, 145, 175

Richard, cold blue eyes. Sharp. They came at you like a switchblade. A challenge, a threat. Best thing to do was ignore, but I smiled. A "you must have kindness in there somewhere" smile, along with a little bit of "you don't frighten me smile" which may be the wrong approach with Richard.

He started out seeming polite with forced communication of polite society. Later, well. Maybe this was an effort for him.

I felt he suspected me of something. What? I don't know. Not a crime. An insult? Was I maybe a threat with my smile in answer to those switchblade eyes?

It was only later I found out he thought I knew his secret. In fact, I did not. Not until later—too late.

Well, chances are he wouldn't have believed me anyway—that was just the way Richard was wired.

In fact, I understand he was not this way as a child—or was he? Maybe the "shy boy" turned into Richard as self-defense against a world that frightened him.

Who knows what happened? Only Richard now and maybe one person. Who though? Who is that person and what is his or her name? Or, is that person still alive? Who knows?

Richard just sits and aims that switchblade gaze at the corner of the Baker-Miller Pink, R(ed): 255, G(reen): 145, B(lue): 175, walls.

KaThunk, KaThunk, KaThunk the boy used his two small hands to dribble the basketball on the concrete drive, slowly approaching the hoop his mother had mounted for him, lower than regulation—he's just a child after all. He furtively glances up and down the block to see if any of the neighbor kids have taken the bait. None of them ever do. Richard is a lonely boy.

I admit, I didn't recognize him. Well, 30 years later? A different name? Why wouldn't I recognize the man who abandoned me deep in the rainforest? I guess left to starve? Die in childbirth? In fact, I gave birth to our little girl, now a woman and we both came out of that rainforest alive and kicking. I don't know what the charge would be—he hadn't murdered anyone; he hadn't kidnapped anyone. What is the crime of abandonment worth?

Unrequited

"OK, Lauren, so tell me why you chose this particular book. Loud and clear please, as you agreed, we are recording this."

Lauren nodded, used her index finger to sweep her hair out of her face and hang it on her right ear. "So, we moved about a year ago. I was mad at myself for not finishing unpacking, especially books, you know. Family books. The day I'd cleared to start going through them was the anniversary of my grandparents. This book was a marriage gift, well, at least according to family stories, a gift from grandaddy Hank to my gamommy Margo on their wedding night."

"Maternal or paternal?"

"Maternal."

Detective Lizbet Golten, took a look at something in a thick and tattered file folder, "Their full names please?"

"Hank Teasdale, Henry, everyone called him Hank, and Margo. Margo Draper before the wedding."

"Well now, I know you've told the story or part of it, but not to me. I have the notes." Here she referred to an iPad rather than the paper file.

Lauren, puzzled, asked, "Two files? And that thick one? It looks old. There is something wrong, or was, wasn't there? Something bad happened. I'm not just letting my imagination run away with me, that, that page…" She stared at the wall behind the detective, her mouth slightly open, her head shaking slowly.

"Lauren, please may I continue the interview?"

"OK"

"First, is this the book you brought into the station?" She tapped a book that was on the desk between them with the tip of a long shapely cobalt blue fingernail. The book was in a plastic bag.

"That looks like it, I don't imagine there are two with the exact same stains or wear."

Detective Golten slipped on a pair of gloves, pulled the book out and opened the book for Lauren, she recognized the odd pencil mark on the remaining page in the front matter and noted the fragments of the other two pages that seemed to have been ripped out. She carefully placed the book back in the bag and took off the gloves. "Probably a useless precaution, a book this old, after all this time. It already has your prints on it, but we might as well mitigate the confusion. It is probably a jumble of prints, nevertheless."

Lizbet Golten looked up her eyebrows implied a question mark. Lauren nodded.

"The book. Yes or no please, Lauren."

"Yes."

Detective Golten narrated for the tape: 2 inches thick, 8 inches tall, 6 inches wide. Hardbound, cloth cover. Faded deep blue green. Two stains of unknown substance. Hardcover slightly warped. The cloth covering the hardcover frayed at the edges. Front and back cover have no lettering. Centered on the front cover is a gold figure, 1 and a quarter inches by same, stylized torch bearer. Back binding torch bearer centered. Above and below are black bands with gold border. Gold lettering. The top reads, centered:

Complete

Poems of

KEATS and SHELLEY

The bottom band reads, centered:

MODERN

LIBRARY

"Now please tell me why you brought this book down to the station today?"

"I opened the cover eager to read the inscription, I was sure, if it was a marriage gift from grandaddy Hank it would have an inscription. It would be like hearing his voice you know, even in writing and what did he say to gamommy? It seemed so romantic. So I, I opened the book in great anticipation only, no inscription, as you see. At least two pages, I'm guessing, just torn out of the book. Only one blank page with that pencil scribble. One page may have had an inscription—it must have, but why? Why torn out? The other page probably had copyright and printing information, maybe they both had inscriptions—I'll never know, I guess. Who did it? It didn't feel right for the word-of-mouth history I had learned of the book. Not for my family, we cherish books. Maybe this wasn't the book. Anyway, after doing a little research of this particular hardcover design I estimate it was printed around 1932. At least the timing would be about right to fit the marriage gift story.

I decided maybe there was an inscription or a special sonnet inside the book that might have been marked, as a special poem for them— well, the romantic in me hoped. I rested the spine on a table and pulled the back and front covers away from each other to let the pages fall where they may. I was hoping it would open to a significant poem. I guess I got significant, but not in the way I imagined. Never...sorry..." Lauren paused, closed her eyes, took a deep breath, blew it out, took a sip of water and continued.

"The book fell to the section of Keats' "Posthumous and Fugitive Poems," though this was not the first thing I noticed. My eyes focused at once on the reason the cover is warped. A boutonnière."

"Excuse me, is this the boutonnière you found in the book?" The detective had produced another plastic bag, this one containing a small yellow and white boutonnière.

Lauren reached for the bag "May I?" The detective handed the bag over. Lauren looked at it from both sides, noting the signs of age and little details. She nodded as she handed it back, then, "Oh, sorry, yes. Anyway, it was all I really noticed. I didn't see the page at first. It was oddly delicate looking, the boutonnière. Small, as though fashioned for a boy not a man. Perhaps the ring bearer? A small yellow rosebud was the focal point. It lay nested on top of small sprays of something white and delicate like little stars with little antenna between. I found out later it is elderflower, a symbol of compassion." Lauren blushed and gave a little snort, "I, well, the yellow rosebud you see, I thought it odd, I think red or white, not yellow for a wedding, so I looked it up— what different rose colors symbolize. Just as I thought, red for true love, white for virtue, purity, but yellow can be so many conflicting things. I made a note," she picked up her iPhone and read, "Friendship, but also jealousy, infidelity, apology, a broken heart, intense emotion, undying love, extreme betrayal. Seems odd for the occasion, right? So, anyway I had to look up elderflower too. Sorry, a bit off track?"

"Please don't worry about it, your reactions may be important, easier to cull out unnecessary information than try to fill in the blanks, especially if we don't know what the blanks are. Please, go on."

"OK, the boutonnière. It still had its pin, also small, well, as you see. I was convinced it was made for a boy. Whose boy? Was he a relative of mine, an uncle? And why save a child's boutonnière? Why not the groom's or a flower from the bride's corsage? And these questions made me realize I've never seen any wedding photos from this side of the family. Why? Finally, I set it aside, curious about the placement of it, it seemed the perfect starting point for reading a book of poems. That is when I noticed the condition of the page. It was more than dog-eared. It was folded back in a complicated manner as though someone decided to try some origami with a fixed flat page, folded in on itself. I carefully unfolded it, I had to lift the page to make sure I didn't tear it. That is when I saw it was cut to pieces. I held my breath, I almost choked. No one in our family would ever cut a book—at least I couldn't imagine it. I felt a chill, it was the creepiest thing I've ever come across. Anyway, I guess I had just seen words against words without reading, but focusing in I saw the words were crooked, made no sense. I realized I was reading partial words with words from the next page showing through. Holes were cut as though with the care and accuracy of an x-acto knife. I felt a real chill then. Why the destruction and why destruction with such surgical accuracy? I had to know, maybe it was a sort of puzzle. I played with guessing the missing words and letters, but the writing—well from such a different time…I found the group of sonnets from that page on the internet to make sure." She picked up her iPhone again, "These were the missing words: grief, snared, tangled, son, dark, waste, cannot look, flight, wrong, barren, sea, thy, haste, bring. And these the letters: b, ers, Th, r, o…" Her voice was starting to quaver.

Detective Golten took advantage of a pause, "No need to complete the list."

"Thank you, I, I felt a little childish, like I watch too many old detective movies. I couldn't help but think of a ransom note, but that made no sense, no sense, a wedding gift…a, my family, sorry." Lauren sat back with a big sigh. She closed her eyes and took another deep breath. Had another sip of water.

Detective Lizbet Golten wanted to pat her hands but refrained. She pulled the thick file folder in front of her, opened it, leafed through the first few pages, then began.

"Did you ever hear of a man named Brady? Jack Brady?"

"No."

"How about, Geoffrey, spelled G e o f f r e y? Geoffrey Teasdale?"

Lauren started and looked up, "Teasdale? My?"

"He was your grandfather's nephew. Did you ever hear that name?"

"Never..."

"You said, no wedding photos, how about any newspapers from 1934?"

"No, not that I ever saw. Old newspapers?"

Detective Lizbet Golten sat up and seemed to weigh her response, "Lauren, we are particularly interested in this book and the boutonnière. You appear to have brought us clues to an old case, an unsolved case, Pop's case." She nodded, "My pop, daddy's little girl followed him into the force. When I was in academy this was all he talked about. It haunted him. I will tell you what I know, but it may be hard for you. Would you like a short break first? Some tea or coffee?"

"No, no, I think knowing is better that leaping from one guess to another. Thank you, please go on."

Detective Lizbet Golten placed her forearms on the table, hands clasped. She no longer needed to refer to the file.

"On your grandparent's wedding day, the little ring bearer, Geoffrey Teasdale, disappeared. He was in the wedding party, wearing this," she picked up the bag with the yellow boutonnière, sat it back down, "and he still had it on at the time the reception started. Now, Jack Brady was your grandfather's best man. Jack, Hank, and Margo were childhood friends, the trio were inseparable. Many people assumed it would be Jack and Margo that would wed, especially Jack. But when Hank and Margo announced their intentions no one seemed as enthused and helpful as Jack. It was Jack that made sure little Geoffy had a boutonnière. Jack designed that boutonnière himself. He hired a chauffeur and arranged an, even then, rare 1930 Bentley 8 Litre, British Racing Green and Black, to whisk the newlyweds away. Now, he also knew about this," she unclasped her hands and again her cobalt blue nails tapped the book in the plastic bag. "He told Hank not to worry about a thing, he'd put it in their honeymoon suite on the ship. Which he did, before disappearing. The boy was never found."

Lauren startled, "Then why do we still have it? Why didn't the police get it?"

Detective Golten, shook her head, "I don't know. Perhaps because of the confusion of the day. Because it was associated with a family tragedy. It may have been kept, but never opened."

"Anyway, when your grandparents climbed into the back seat, they found centered in the seat, the boutonnière and an envelope marked "Urgent" in cutout letters. This was inside that envelope." She pulled something from the file, also in plastic, and placed it in front of Lauren. The note began, in cutout letters: "if you want to sea your brother's son again…"

Innocence

She wiped my gaze off the back of her head. Hand lingering, barely brushing back and forth as if distracted by the feel of the newly close-cropped hair. That color neither blonde nor brunette. It must darken in winter and turn toward blonde in summer. This being spring it showed pinpoints of blonde on burnished brown. Her pace slowed, left foot hovering gently over the polished marble before making contact, and resuming her pace across the lobby toward the concierge desk. At night is this grand hallway crawling with immigrants, a chamois in each hand or does it echo as a couple of guys waltz around each other with their 475-pound industrial floor polishers?

Not quite sure which ruse to try I went straight to the person who'd given a room access card to Might-Be-Della"—my missing cousin, given up for dead twenty years ago.

"Hello! Welcome to The Palace Hotel, your name please?"

"Greer..."

"Oh! Dr. Greer, we are glad you could make it for the convention after all. How lucky we've not released your room yet. I am surprised your assistant didn't call us back right away. But excuse me, yes, we still have your room, top floor away from the elevator and ice machine."

Who was I to correct this happy accident? I'd sort out paying the credit card bill later. What if mom had not been a huge Greer Garson fan? Yes, Greer really is my name and it was fabulous not going to school with other little Greers running around, no teacher had to try to come up with working nicknames for us. I shudder to think what those might have been.

Now here I was, a guest at The Palace Hotel, historic landmark in the great city of San Francisco. I had toyed with the idea of stopping here to ask the concierge if I could stash my rucksack for the day. I had planned an in-and-out visit. Coast Starlight train down, head over to the deYoung Legion of Honor Museum at Lincoln Park to see KLIMT & RODIN: An Artistic Encounter, stop for dinner here at the Pied Piper Bar & Grill, Coast Starlight back. I cannot explain my fascination and love for Klimt, it was there in my gut, seeing his images made me smile and now here was a chance to see thirty of his works for the first time ever on the West Coast. Not only that, right here in San Francisco, a city I conjure excuses to visit. My last trip was several years ago to walk the Golden Gate Bridge on her 75th Anniversary.

I left the train station and made my way to Montgomery Street, undecided whether to walk to The Palace Hotel to stash my rucksack for the day or to grab the 38R and head straight for Lincoln Park. California and Montgomery, that's where I first clapped eyes on her. A brief profile as she made the corner and fell into step ahead of me on the sidewalk. I almost cried out "Dell!" I restrained myself, I lectured myself that I must have been thinking about her and let my imagination get the better of me but Wow! her pace matched mine perfectly like when we were kids. Her upright posture with that funny quirky motion of her right hand, fingers splayed in the backward curve of her funky loose joints. We were close cousins. People, said we seemed like twins, well I felt almost as devastated as a twin might when she disappeared.

"Thin air." I remember the adults repeating those words, parents, teachers, neighbors. I remember taking deep breaths to see if it felt thin to me. The police never said that. They asked questions, scribbled notes, asked more questions, talked into their radios. I wondered when they were going to ask me questions and what they would ask. Seemed like I waited a long time. Then another car arrived with a woman, a policewoman, I was something special I guess because she only questioned me. She knelt down, softened her voice introduced herself, Officer Peña, Gloria Peña. I'll never forget her name, her voice, the way her short ponytail seemed to sneak down the collar of her shirt, her Chanel.

Della and I both had long hair, it was still floaty and soft like baby hair and rarely looked combed, we loved to play outside no matter the weather, we ignored dolls and spent our time digging foxholes, seeking clues to some unknown mystery that we never clearly defined, collecting leaves and globes of amber pitch off trees and riding our 3-speed bikes all over town—it was a small town. It isn't always the big scary city where bad things happen. That's what I figured out when Della disappeared.

I knew from reading leCarré not to follow too closely so I slowed my pace, looked around, enjoyed the weather, listened to the street whistles signaling the presence of tourists in the neighborhood. I made sure to wear a look of confidence and strength. I felt pretty stealthy until I followed her into the Palace. Watched her check in and walk toward the Concierge. I guess I got a little too close and gazed a little too long. I broke off before she lowered her hand and looked around. I settled in a lobby chair and affected a business-like air as I pulled my Kate Spade purse out of the rucksack, unzipped the flap to expose my iPad and pulled up the Palace guest wi-fi.

Might-be-Della turned from the Concierge a brochure with hotel details and a city map in hand. She wandered into the Garden Court dining area, admired the glass dome, the architectural details, but then she wandered behind potted plants and slowly walked the perimeter of the room, pausing occasionally to look more closely at what I don't know—the baseboards? Done there she came out, turned right and headed around toward the Grand Ballroom and Regency Foyer. If memory serves, she'd certainly see me if I followed and she'd have to come back this way, so I waited. And waited, too long. I could wait no more. I attempted to wear the look of another guest looking at the rooms and the display cases of memorabilia from the hotel's history. I checked the rooms, Grand, Gold, Regency. I checked the restrooms. It was like twenty years ago. She'd vanished into thin air. No, somehow, I just missed her. I resigned myself to patience enforced by going up to my room, dropping my stuff, such as it was, off and grabbing a bus to see the Klimt and Rodin. Which is what I did.

I returned through the Market Street door in time to see Might-Be-Della slipping out the door of the not quite yet opened Pied Piper. The way she hiked her shoulder and cut the door jamb close I was more certain than ever it was Dell but I was too jazzed from coming face-to-face with "Ria Munk III," "The Virgin," and the haunting gaze of the unfinished "Portrait of a Lady." I was tired. I went to my room to stretch and clean up and have an inspiration about Might-Be-Della before coming back down to dine in view of Parrish's "Pied Piper of Hamelin" hung behind the bar.

I woke early, restless, was down before the Garden Court opened for breakfast. Pacing the grand hallway lobby area like a snow leopard I dropped my chin to get lost in the patterns in the natural marble floor. Midway to The Pied Piper the sheen off the marble floor was interrupted by patches of dullness. At first, I thought the nightly cleaning crew had missed some spots but no, the dull patches were all of the same size and there was a regularity, a pattern to them. Curious I stopped and moved around to get different perspective on them and finally I saw them for what they were, prints. Footprints heading my way, faint shadows on the marble but as I backtracked them to their origin, they gained definition as dried, muddy Vibram Eton soled shoe prints. Mud. The Palace Hotel. Downtown San Francisco. The incongruity was pushed to the background by the shock of those prints. I recognized the circles left by the Eton Vibram sole because I was wearing a pair of shoes with the same soles myself. They are ideal for shoes like the Spectus designed for posture control. As cousins Della and I shared more than interests, friendship, and play. We shared genetic back issues that required corrective devices including shoes. It is what gave us both our almost military posture and distinctive gait. I turned around and hovered my right foot over a right print...a match. Dell. Had to be. The prints came out of the Pied Piper close cropping the doorway like I'd seen Might-Be-Della the day before. I peeked inside, mud on the carpet, much more easily seen, came from the service hallway behind the bar.

I heard voices and smelled coffee. The Garden Court was open for breakfast. I asked for a perimeter table tucked in next to one of the potted palms and ordered huevos rancheros and coffee. In she came, choosing the buffet she was seated with her back to me. I had another cup of coffee to give her time to eat then I got up and took the chair opposite her.

"Dell..."

"No, no..." she whispered without shaking her head. Our eyes were locked, and I knew this was Della. I felt like a missing part of my soul was restored and how many women my age and height have a gold spot in their blue left eye?

"Dell, cousin...it's me."

"No, I can't know you, not now I'm so close. Leave, please leave Greer." Ah those silent tears, she always fought them.

"Let me help, you know I can't leave. Where were you last night?"

"Last night?"

"You tracked mud in."

Her posture faded for a moment; her chin dropped. "I guess I was too frustrated, I know better."

"Let's get out. We'll take the 5 Fulton to the park. Yes?"

So, we paid for our meals and agreed to meet in the lobby in 20 minutes. It was Dell alright, and now that she'd accepted my presence, I was confident she'd meet me there.

She was quiet on the bus; we both did our fair share of people watching.

Once we got to the park and started walking, our old habits kicked in. I had to walk on her left to avoid that funny right arm circle in her walk, our strides were still well-matched. She started to talk. She still had the intensity I remember but her lightness was—not gone I hoped—but buried under secrets and pain.

"My little niece..."

"But Dell, she doesn't even know you, your family doesn't..."

"My new family...MY family...my niece, she went missing 7 months ago. I imagine it was like me—after a period of time she was presumed dead, not legally but you could see it in their eyes, her mom and dad and brother. Everyone. She became past tense or non-existent in conversation. I never accepted it. Well, you know," she almost snorted, held her arms out looked down at them and hugged herself, "look at me. I'm here, not dead. I come over from Grass Valley periodically looking. I feel like she's here. I peruse blogs and Flickr, Instagram, the news. I recently came across a BMXer blog about riding the tunnels in underground San Francisco. There were lots of pictures. One of them, well it had an old upended peddler's cart against a wall of graffiti and trash in mud and I swear when I expanded the trash I could make out the outline of a pencil box, faded, partially covered in mud, but I swear it had a fawn on it, there was still green in the background and it might have been a cloud above but I think it was Godzilla's foot. Shoo-Shoo loved her little "Bambi Meets Godzilla" pencil box. She carried it everywhere. If I could just find it maybe there would be other clues. I've made a lot of attempts and accessed tunnels from various areas. This area is one of my last. The bloggers don't want to ruin a good thing so aren't specific about where their pictures were taken. I come once a month. I try different entry points. Last week I came across a comment from someone involved in the restoration of The Palace. There are huge rooms under the hotel. I found a way down last night through The Pied Piper, but it took me awhile and I tripped over something and lost my flashlight. I have to go back."

"Of course, we do Dell. But...I...what happened? Where did you go? Why didn't you come back? What is this about your new family? I don't understand."

"You won't ever be able to understand. I don't. And until I find Shoo-Shoo—Annabelle's nickname (don't ask). Until I find her, I'm not saying anything, maybe never will Greer. I was snagged. I survived after a fashion. Maybe Shoo-Shoo will fare as well, maybe better, please I hope better. You won't call them? Anyone? Please don't, you won't, you can't—I can't. Remember? Pals forever no matter what? Well that became complicated for me from down here. It was a long way from Seattle for an eleven-year-old—that's how old I was when I got away. But now that we're together again: pals no matter what OK?"

We walked the length of the park east to west and crossed the Great Highway. Took off our matching shoes and walked barefoot across the sand to stand in the Pacific. Side-by-side again in that comfortable silence between friends, cousins. I got cold first, I always did. We sat on a wall against the sidewalk, air dried our feet, and put socks and shoes back on. Headed up Fulton to catch the 5 back. We spotted a Safeway between Cabrillo and Fulton set back from La Playa. We bought flashlights, towels, water for our urban spelunking. Waiting for the bus we figured that since the Pied Piper closed at midnight, we'd go in for a late snack at 11:30, at last call for alcohol we'd slip into the restrooms and hang out until staff cleared the decks.

We weren't sure if anyone ever did a thorough check of restrooms before closing so we were ready to crouch atop toilet seats if need be.

Things got quiet. No one ever came in to clear the restroom. I followed Dell down the service hall between the bar and dining area. She opened a janitor's closet, leading with her right foot she did her funny shoulder fold and stepped inside around the swab bucket. She turned the flashlight beam to a seam in the back wall, slipped a file in and pried open a hatch that revealed a set of stairs and a cavernous darkness until she filled it with her flashlight beam. Down she went and I followed.

It was quiet, cold, a little damp. There were more stairs than I expected. The floor was damp and dirty it seemed like concrete that had been flooded multiple times leaving a cushioning layer of mud in the low spots. We swept the room with light revealing steam engines presumably from the early 1900s. Early Palace power. We retrieved Dell's lost flashlight. Marveled at these ancient elegant machines and continued on our way. We headed for an opening that we thought must be under New Montgomery Street. The graffiti looked promising, we pushed on. Then Dell saw it. A pushcart. She scanned down with her light, stiffened, reached down and swatted away dust and debris with a towel revealing a little patch of green, a fawn. Using the same towel, she picked up the pencil box she had given Annabelle. She was barely breathing as she opened the box. Inside were two mechanical pencils. One of the tiny slips of paper that came with the box had writing on it. Tears poured down Dell's face as she stared at the note. I looked over her shoulder.

"Auntie Dell, I'm sorry for whatever I've done wrong. I love you all. Tell mommy and daddy, Shoo-Shoo wants to come home."

Lookout

Seeking my "mad place" I tiptoed the Montero carefully up the heavily rutted road.

Look where you want to go. Look where you want to go. Look where you want to go. I repeated my mantra learned from 20 years of motorcycling. This kept my eyes on the route ahead navigating bends, curves, ruts and, more importantly, prevented target fixation on the precipice and the long lonely drop below.

Yojimbo let out a low half growl from his securely belted carrier.

"Good kitty, Yojimbo. We must be getting close. Good kitty." This was wishful thinking. The farther and longer I wound up through the forest and up the mountain, picking my way between a steep slope looming over me on one side and an equally steep drop on the other, the more I questioned what I was doing. There was no sign of another vehicle, or a fellow biped of any kind for the last two hours. Rather than a hoped-for relief, this brought on a loneliness tinged with self-doubt— what had I gotten myself into? I started down the road of anxiety. I heard a stranger's voice beginning to speak "Be careful what you wish for my pretty....ahhhh ha ha ha ha..." Oh my god! Miss Gulch! I hear the Miss Gulch/Wicked Witch music as she pedals away in the whipping wind.

"STOP!" I yell.

"Brrrt?" Yojimbo-speak for "what's up?" Followed by one of those audible cat yawns and a bit of a head shake.

"Good kitty, good kitty"...time to 'put my sad down' that's all. I stop (neutral, hand break on), plug my phone back in and shuffle my anti-depressant playlist. Still stopped, I turn to look in the back at the Forest

Service VHF radio I just picked up a few hours ago, my many gallons of water, thermal food chest, a box of dried and canned goods including cat food, and a Big Bag of dried bonito flakes for Yojimbo, boots, backpack, boxes full of books, notebooks, and refills for my mechanical pencil, spare batteries of many shapes and sizes, flashlight, the recently purchased sheets, blankets, pillow in addition to my sleeping bag. What had I forgotten?

"OK Yojimbo, won't be long now." I put the Montero back into gear, released the brake and continue upward.

"Approximately June 1 through September 30 depending on seasonal changes" the job description said. The word 'remote' was used several times, the fifth word in to be precise. "Duties: Serves as a remote lookout in the detection of wildland fires." ... "must be independent" and bring in own food and water to last "at least 14 days at a time."

I have a fascination for fire lookouts—both the structures and the people manning them: I had a cousin, my cousin Grace, who did this every summer since she was old enough to apply. I never knew her very well, not sure anyone did. People didn't understand her love for this job, she heard all the stereotypical jargon "Why would such a beauty hide herself away every summer looking for fires? How is she ever going to find a good husband?" I was quite a bit younger than her, just old enough to join her brother in trying to frighten her, her older sister and my big sister with jointed wooden snakes and rubber snakes, rubber spiders and the occasional fake rat. I remember them jumping and screaming but now I wonder whether we really "got them" or if they were just being good sports and letting the little kids have their fun.

I kinda had a romantic fascination with my hero cousin saving trees and Bambi and all his forest friends from wildfires. As an adult I had an unanticipated close encounter with a burn as we headed east in the night...we were one of the last cars through as the fire crews were getting ready to shut the highway down as the fire threatened jumping across it. Nothing can compare to that image of the land ablaze as far as I could see, heightened by the contrast of the glow against the night sky. Then I read Timothy Egan's *The Big Burn*. It all added up to the idea growing of trying it some time. That idea became more appealing when I walked out on my job one day, notice given, vacation taken, I planned never to set foot in the place again. A micromanager had taken over and I, for a time, tried to adjust and cope and make it work. Then after three of my coffee buddies and support crew got fed up and left, there I was feeling lost and alone. I was becoming an angry bitter person that I no longer recognized. I yelled at cars that rolled crosswalks as I was about to cross where I used to shrug my shoulders or even laugh or think, *Wow...if it's that important to ya I'm sure sorry for ya.*

It seemed like the perfect time to check out the job of fire lookout. It would be pretty hard to micro-manage a lookout it seemed. Remoteness was icing on the cake. Maybe my geography background will help me get the job, I hoped—I worried about it. There must be people chomping at the bit for these jobs and they are becoming scarce as lookouts are decommissioned and sometimes burned down—now there is irony—and as other techniques are being relied on rather than the live lookouts. Numbering in the hundreds now rather than the thousands hired in the days between the Big Burn of 1910 and the end of WWII.

I was lucky, the tower I'm assigned to has road access all the way up. Some, lookouts are dropped by helicopter or have to hike in and hike in and hike in. Well, I would have brought far fewer things if I had to make multiple trips up a trail, as it is, I will have to get everything up a ladder. I'll leave my books down in the car and take them up as I need them. My Montero will serve as my own personal bookmobile.

Three songs later we broke tree line and for the first time except in a Forest Service photo shown me when I met my boss, I saw our summer house, a room, called a "cab", mounted atop tall lodge poles, with a wrap-around porch accessible via ladder. It literally took my breath away and I stopped to stoop over the wheel and get my nose closer to the windshield for a better view. Thrilling, in multiple senses of the word. Excitement, hope, promise, fear, regret, trepidation. Back in gear I continued the last few hundred yards which revealed the base of the tower and the dreaded outhouse. I pulled up and had a mental block about where to park then realizing I was overthinking it I did the practical first step of backing up closer to the base of the tower near the ladder. I got out and walked around to unbelt Yojimbo's carrier and move it from the seat to the ground. "Welcome home Yojimbo!" Every which way I looked was a landscape waiting to be photographed, painted, remembered and to the south bigger than life, Mt. Hood, our next-door neighbor.

I looked up at our living quarters and the ladder, *How am I going to get Yojimbo up there? The litter?* That was probably the heaviest item. I hoped for a 'dumb waiter' and was relieved to see one. The wood box looked sturdy enough, but who knows, it could be rotted, and the rope seemed suspect to me. I was glad I threw in that coil of Geoff's rope he offered me, and I still had my knot tying instruction app on my phone from when I was taking sailing lessons. I wished I'd been a star at knot tying but I didn't put in the practice time. With an internal flip of a switch brain churn ceased and I flew up the ladder. "Be right back kitty!" I had to see where we'd be spending the next four months. After all I had all kinds of time to unload and set up housekeeping.

The screen door made this a luxury lookout and as a bonus it had a proper screen door hinge song just like on Granmommy Schwinn's house. I unlocked the glass paned door and stepped inside. Pride of place the 360-degree view. Everywhere I turned was a view every realtor would crave to list—in spades. No freeway, no clear cut, no shopping mall. I was too new to it to see the trails and access roads that I later learned were there. I never knew so many shades of green the landscape held, changing with elevation from valley to peak, a glint and a line of poplar and willow hinted at a river or stream, and then so close I wanted to reach out and pet it, Mt. Hood. My self-doubt went the way of my breath.

I HAD found my "Mad Place". My tree stump on the hill above my childhood home was my sanctuary. When the world was not going my way, I stomped up the hill with Lana, the beagle that was raising me, trotting happily behind, nose to the ground tail in the air wagging. She snaked around my legs to trot ahead, jumped on the stump, turned around and half-bayed at me. As soon as I was settled into this throne, fit for a good pout Lana was off in the underbrush sniffing and wagging and circling back to check in on me. It was here I could smell the scents of the various trees and, depending on the time of year, the lilac blooming by the side of our garage. I could see across my little hometown and across the docks, my dad's office, the Black Ball dock, the spit, the paper mill, the marina and the Strait of Juan de Fuca. On a clear day I could see Canada. It was here I found calm. It was here anger, anxiety, sadness slipped away leaving me whole. I learned years later my mom knew exactly where I was and how healing it was for me. Should my sister or dad or neighbor or friend ask my whereabouts mom would drawl that "Little Betz has gone to her mad place." The precious thing is she did not divulge its precise whereabouts. Of course, my dad and sister knew, they too seemed to know that I needed this quiet time and space.

"Brrooooowwww! Brrrt. Brrrt. Brroooouuuwwww!"

"I'll be right down Yoji!" I could see his cat-cringe at my using this nickname not of his own choosing.

Back down on the ground self-doubt crept over me like a shadow. *How am I going to get Yojimbo up there safely? Will my knees handle all the trips? There is no way Yojimbo will stand for being zipped up in my backpack or me making a front sling. I don't know if I trust the dumb waiter and that rope... How am I going to get all my gear up there? What if there's a fire right now and I don't see it,*

I'm not ready and can't interpret the Osborne Firefinder correctly? What if I send wrong coordinates? What if my radio doesn't work?...OK OK OK. Deep breaths, smile, look around. Stop making up a melodramatic story. Remember Anne Lamott: "Bird by Bird". OK, I'll take care of Yojimbo first.

The dumb waiter might be my second-best friend up here next to Yojimbo. Rather than assuming it isn't sound I walked over to inspect it. A box, a wooden oblong box, well weathered and it looked the right dimension to accommodate the cat carrier. The two narrow sides were taller than the long sides and narrowed to a rounded point at the top in which a one-inch diameter whole was drilled and sanded smooth. It was through these the suspect rope was strung. I picked it up by the rope. There was a slight resistance against the soil it had settled into. The lifting of it disturbed a colony of saw bugs and centipede-like critters that all seemed to cringe and squint and scurry for cover of a nearby rock. Weathered yes and damp on the bottom yes but the wood itself seemed sound and solid, cedar maybe? The box was well made, meant to last more than a single season. The rope, I wish I knew more about rope. It felt like it might be OK, just stained and dirty but I didn't want to test it with Yojimbo, nor was I confident I could tie a replacement securely. I decided to test it with the litter box and kitty litter. The litter box just fit, and I hefted the bag of litter into it, released the rope from its anchor and started to haul hand over hand. Nothing seemed to snap or fray. I was pleased to see guide wires that kept the dumb waiter from swinging to and fro. The box rose up through its hole in the decking and I anchored it off, climbed up the ladder and unloaded. I looked at the rope, the pulleys it all looked OK to my novice eye so back down the ladder I went, released the rope and brought the dumb waiter back to ground.

"OK Yojimbo."

"Prrrrrt?"

"Ready for a ride up?"

No answer. I hoisted his carrier onto the box—a perfect fit.

"Ride-a-ticcy!"

This was my singsong when Yojimbo was happily settled on one of our office chairs and I had to wheel it out of the way of something. Using the same hand over hand method as before I slowly hoisted Yojimbo up the side of the lookout tower. I could see his face pressed against the peepholes of his carrier. I was pretty sure his tail was low and swaying side-to-side. One more success, but I was shocked at how out of shape I was, weak hands and my upper body strength was worrisome considering that I needed to haul up radio, water, and food. I might have to move in partially today—use a sleeping bag tonight and set up housekeeping tomorrow.

Back up the ladder, I carried Yojimbo into our cab, made sure all the door and window screens were in place and started unlatching the carrier clasps, as I reached the eighth and final clasp Yoji shifted slightly in anticipation. I lifted the lid and he sat up tall and silent and still except for his whiskers and nose. Sniff, sniff, sniff. Then his big green eyes began the circuit. Sniffing and scanning the room he stood up and slowly, one big paw at a time he stepped out of his carrier. Yojimbo is a big muscular Maine Coon cat with bronzed tiger stripes, a coral colored nose, and belly fur almost apricot, with white booted rear paws. I love watching him from behind. He has a way of rotating those big shoulders and when he cleans himself his left paw comes all the way to the back of his neck and then he rubs his own head and a little shoulder jook reminiscent of Toshiro Mifune in many of his characters working with Akira Kurosawa, hence my cat's name. Cats will take their time getting to know a place, so I busied myself setting up his litter box just behind the open door. Phuphump! I heard Yoji jump up onto something. I turned to look and there he was sitting in the exact center of the Osborne Fire Finder table, right where our lookout is shown.

I took better stock of the contents of the cab and petting Yojimbo worked out priorities for what to bring up before nightfall and what could wait for tomorrow. Water, food, tools of my new trade: binoculars, VHF radio. My hands were already stinging a little from the rope. It was on my way down the ladder that I remembered that just at the last minute I'd thrown in a pair of my trusty Ace Hardware all-round work/ gardening gloves. I heard Joni and called out "I am a geeeeenious!" with a big smile on my face. Funny how big a spike in mood the little things can make. This kept me going long enough to get what I considered first night essentials up from the car and an early start at settling in. As I worked the light changed to a warm glow and soon, I was enjoying the light of the waning gibbous moon, still bright. I was enamored with being able to see so well by moonlight—pure moon and starlight. And how many stars!!! Why spoil this experience of living by moonlight and seeing all these stars when I was used to being able to only make out Orion and the Bears. Dark here is really dark—no ambient city light, not even any rural light. The first twinkles of light, like semaphore ship to ship signals, presumably a by-product of wind and trees, were miles away.

The wind picked up, I could see wisps of snow dust blowing like scarves around the neck of Mt. Hood in the moonlight, then a wash of dimness as the first cloud born out of seemingly nowhere obscured the moon briefly. The wind blew in through the window and door screens, so I closed the door and most of the windows and pulled on a fleece hoodie. Meanwhile Yojimbo, one of those cats that love the wind, was sitting at the window of the kitchen or should I call it a galley? The blue grays of the moonlight and his shape made an iconic watercolor portrait. His tail up and swishing made a companion to his body. Ears alert I knew his eyes must be aglow. This is why I closed almost, but not all the shutters. How could I shut out Yoji's world toy? Before I knew it, more clouds flew between me and the moon. The light flickered like an old black and white movie reel gone off its tracks. I didn't know the layout well and in the dark/light I became disoriented and couldn't locate my flashlight or the lanterns.

Suddenly it seemed I was watching one of those fast forward sequences demonstrating a swift weather change. I saw the first flush of lightening way off at the horizon. I held my breath but forgot to count waiting for the low rumble to follow. Wait, wait I need to breathe. Phew—then like muffled timpani came the thunder. I remember my mom calming me during thunder and lightning storms she had a "magic insulating pillow" for me and we watched, and she pointed out all the beauty of the phenomenon. I now recognize the beauty of storms, but I still have a core of anxiety about them. I hope I won't need my Alprazolam as I'm not sure I can find it now in the mostly dark. I watched the lightening walk its way closer and closer. Spectacular, I've never witnessed anything quite like this. The timpani became more pronounced; no more muffling. Long rolls now and I could feel them vibrating in my gut. Was the cab vibrating a bit too? I looked at Yojimbo. He is one of those cats—when the Blue Angels thunder overhead he looks up with a fed-up look and proceeds to clean his nether parts. He was not perturbed by this light show.

As the lightning struck closer and closer advancing toward us an avalanche of questions spewed forth in my mind.

Wait! How dry is it? Why don't I remember? What if it sets a blaze? What if it strikes the cab and sets us ablaze? What if I really can't find the flashlight? The lanterns, the radio? What if I can't read the Osborne correctly? Whaaaaa? CRACK! Immediately the timpani rolled. I could feel the electricity, my hair actually crackled and frizzed. That looked like it struck just outside!

OK Betz, deep breaths, use the light flashes to orient, not disorient. Crackle flash rumble. *Don't leave this spot, just scan with each flash and then rotate OK?* Crackle flash rumble. *You cannot control the weather.* Crackle flash rumble. *Use the light. Rotate scan again.* It seemed as though once the storm was upon us, rather than continuing to pass through it decided to stay for a visit. Long crackling bright flashes shaking rolling rumbling LOUD thunder. It was the hair-raising crackling that was the worst. *OK I'll never be annoyed by the people at the play sitting behind me opening their cellophane-wrapped candy.* Crackle flash rumble. Shaking, heart racing, teeth uncontrollably and arrhythmically clacking. My face must look like a gargoyle in the bright flashes. White white blue white light followed by thick impenetrable velvet black. *Even if I do find my flashlight and Alprazolam*—those were top of mind—*it is too late for the alprazolam now, nonsense! Now I was arguing with myself.*

"MmmrROW!" Yoji! Circling comforting. I picked him up, SNAP! We sparked each other then I received an immediate forehead-butt and face rubs accompanied by deep steady purring as if to say, "It is OK you are my family, my person, we'll be OK, breathe, breathe, breathe." I held this densely muscled-cat body close and buried my face in his thick fur, wetting it with tears. His big bottle brush tail coiled around my arm. The lightening moved on; the thunder faded into the distance. My heart rate headed toward normal, my teeth settled down. Finally, I held Yoji out so we were looking eye to eye and said through a post-cry grin "Now we'll have some peace and quiet in this town."

I did a little sway and kissed Yoji right between his ears and sat him down on the Osborne.

"OK, Yojimbo, we've got a job to do and I don't need the flashlight or lantern in order to do it." In fact, I figured being in the dark gave me an advantage in spotting misplaced flickers of light that could indicate a lightning strike setting off a blaze. I took a deep breath and scanned, turning this time with my focus out beyond our little cab scanning to the horizon looking out. That twinkle there, I'll come back to it but I'm pretty sure that's the little town I'll be able to restock supplies from in about 14 days, but I'll come back to it. The radio had no strike reports from other lookouts. I spent a quiet 45 minutes scanning 360 degrees. No change to the flicker. No other lookouts reporting anything either that might need confirming or triangulation. I decided to use my fresh training to confirm—or deny—that the flickers were what and where I guessed. It would be good practice. I stood up tall. I smiled, I felt almost giddy. I'd gone from terror to doing my job. And suddenly I remembered exactly where I'd set the flashlight down. I could now get the lanterns going and get settled in for my first night's read and sleep high above tree line, Yojimbo and Mt. Hood my bunkmates.

I awoke the next morning to a bird symphony composed of new and familiar birdsong and gentle paw patting on my face. Yojimbo, my faithful alarm clock. The cab glowed with the first blush of the sun. Yojimbo and I nuzzled foreheads and I got up donning an extra pair of socks and my fleece hoodie and thought of actor Jimmy Stewart's "Aberdaire you're beautiful, but Aberdaire you're cold."

"OK Yoji, what'll it be this morning? Kibble?" That got me the Jack Benny look.

"Mackerel and sweet potato?"

"Prrrrt." Yoji's that'll suffice in a pinch.

"Want to share eggs with me?"

"MrrrreOW! MrrrreOW! MrrrreOW!"

After breakfast I did some dusting and sweeping then transferred my worldly goods of the summer up to the cab and set up our home. I sat outside for a while on the wrap around walkway, legs swing in out over the edge and lifted my face to the sun and smiled. I hadn't smiled in a great while and it felt both strange and good.

I thought about a soft spot I'd found in the decking while sweeping. How bad was it? Could I repair it? Why not? I've never done that kind of thing before, but I can learn. I'll need some planks; I'll take a look around I know some things are stocked from previous repair and maintenance projects.

I looked up just in time to see a magpie landing on the rail quite near. I heard Yojimbo's jaw loosening sound, as did the magpie who called back in dissonant tones. Yojimbo spoke back through the screen, tail contemplative and sweeping the floor of the cab, the magpie ruffled its wings and stroked the deck rail with its beak before answering. Yojimbo switched from jaw loosening sounds to his curious speaking voice and thus began a summer long friendship between the two. By summer's end the two could be seen sitting/perched side by side on the deck rail facing out to the horizon or Mt. Hood, Yoji's bottle brush tail hanging down elegant and almost imperceptibly swaying, Bartok, as I'd begun calling the magpie, occasionally adjusting his harlequin tail feathers with a quiet swish. I wondered what their conversation entailed but I was not privy so didn't pry, though I have many a photo of this pair.

Over the course of the summer our fire lookout became home to Yojimbo and I. Our friends and neighbors were countless in the wildlife. Yoji became even more muscular and quite adept at the ladder. He almost caught a ground squirrel when suddenly the poor thing went from "flight" to "freeze". Yoji looked puzzled then took on the role of mentor gently pushing at the little thing with his huge soft paw, claws furled. "Maow." Pat pat pat "prrrt maow". Trying his best in cat/squirrel communication to explain that the game called for the squirrel to continue to run so Yoji could continue the chase.

I got to know my lookout-mates by voice, inflection and radio-speak style—we had a friendly competition going of first to spot and radio in a fire—I learned how to replace rotten decking and make various other repairs around the tower. I met several hikers and conversed with some in makeshift sign language as they spoke little English and I spoke little French and even less Swedish—"je ne comprends pas; oui; fermer la vache" the extent of my French and the latter from Honkworm's "Fish of War" episode—and I learned "Tack" from watching Wallander. I developed strength I never suspected I was capable of and although I used sunscreen judiciously my skin reflected a glow from fresh air and sunshine.

I reported fire-starts and helped triangulate fires reported by my fellow lookouts to the East and North. I learned to tell the difference between dust raised by logging operations, a phenomenon of fog seeming to rise from pinpoint locations and real smoke. I experienced a few more literally hair-raising lightning storms and I admit I never relished them, but I learned to accept and endure them and be watchful for strikes without a thought about Alprazolam.

Suddenly September drew to a close and it was time to pack up and secure the cab for the fall and winter. I made one last batch of the pancakes that we shared with Bartok usually on Sundays, packed the Montero and went back up the ladder for a final check and lockup. As I left, I heard myself say "Bye little cab, see you in June!" Of course, I had already made arrangements to sign on as a lookout next season— no guarantee I'd be assigned the same tower, but chances were good. In the end I'd go where needed and would learn a new cab and terrain if necessary, but the life of a summer lookout was in my blood.

The Four "Gs" Of Martha Rae

I once loved the quiet days where I had even a few moments to myself, it was hard to be alone with one sister and four brothers, not to mention living in a small close-knit town. Don't get me wrong, I love this kind of town we are in and out of each other's houses, always ready to lend a hand, share some food, the screen doors screak and bang, someone calls out who it is and what they're doing:

Screak, slam, "Y'all! Just Ruby Ellen, momma said to bring you some of her fresh chocolate pixie cookies." Screak, slam and she was gone again. Like that. Friendly, open.

Anyway, yes, I did once cherish the quiet times—it didn't feel like isolation then—and it never lasted more than but a few hours at most and that was rare, I tell you what.

Now? Not now, no. I long for family, friends, neighbors. At my age there just aren't many about that, no, well truth be told no one that knows me like a childhood friend or sibling knows a person. No one that shares the same or similar history or experiences. Don't get me wrong, I'm lucky and glad to be alive and healthy at my 110 years— what would momma and daddy make of it? I lost the last of my cats to age some months ago. If one finds me and needs me, I'll take it in and love it and feed it. Frankly I don't know how much time there is left to me now, I'm told I'm about 1 in 1,000. I don't mean this as doom and gloom, no, it's just the numbers I expect.

There's the screen door now, screak, bang, I stayed in the other room and picked up my mask just in case whoever it was came in. They weren't supposed to, but people like to see people don't they now?

"Bags are on the table Mizz Martha. You'll want to put the frozen away soon, it's hotting up real good and fast today." Ah, the grocer's son.

"Much obliged Ronnie, don't forget your envelope…"

"Now Mizz Martha you don't need to do that."

"Go ahead and take it son, you don't need to do what you're doing either."

We both chuckled.

"Yes'm. If you need anything before next week you just call now, hear?"

"Bye bye Ronnie, and you keep that mask on or I'll turn you over my knee and paddle you!"

"Yes, MAM!"

Screak, slam. I listened to Ronnie's boots across the porch, jumping down the steps, a door slam and his grandad's old Studebaker pickup start up and fade away out of the neighborhood. It is supposed to be a scorcher today. May as well get up and into the kitchen to put the frozen and sundry away.

What now? I believe I'll go out and sit on the porch awhile to rock and ruminate before the sun comes 'round this side of the house. The wood of the porch is still warm from yesterday. Feels good on my feet, familiar. I was born in this house a late-breaking surprise. I took my first steps out here on these same boards. A course it's had a new coat of paint or two.

Not much to watch these days, the neighbor kids aren't allowed to play together right now, there's no traffic to speak of except Ronnie on his deliveries and old Doc Homer's hearse. He's not really a doctor, "Doc" is short for Doctorow. Land's sakes I don't know what Rosie and Franklin were thinking when they hung that name on a tiny baby,

Doctorow Winslow Homer. Well, didn't seem to do him any harm. No cats to join me unless one of the neighbor cats happens along as they sometimes do…stop on their rounds to pay old Miss Martha a visit.

I sat down in the old rocking chair, best in the world to my mind anyway. Weren't much to look at. Daddy rocked me in this very rocker before the war and the flu and the deaths. My older brothers and sister would tease me ruthlessly—how I missed that—still do. I—we, momma and I, lost them all, daddy included, on foreign soil—all but Beau, the youngest but me, and we lost him crossing the Atlantic on a troop ship headed over. Dropped dead except the ship was so crowded with boys and men that he just kinda slid between the legs of his mates like a wet noodle. At least that's the way his best mate Jeb described it in his letter to us. We still have that letter and five more letters or telegrams with black borders in an old cigar box. I was eight years old and momma and I were at a loss how to comfort each other, but we managed somehow.

Poor Jeb. That's a sad case, they say he "survived" the war. I don't know about that. He came home, I'll grant you that, but most of the time he just sat and stared. Many years later the boys who came back from Viet Nam called it the thousand-yard stare. People now call what ailed him survivor's guilt and PTSD. He lived a ripe old age himself. Some say when he finally passed that it was a mercy.

They all went to fight the Great War. Daddy, Hank, Dooley, Boone, Beauregard, sweet Beau. Daddy always said momma named him that because he refused to buy her a bloodhound. Even Annie May wouldn't be stopped from going over. Well, she had the training and the skills, she was one of hundreds of nurses doing active duty in French field hospitals. The things they must have seen. We lost them all to the three "Gs": guns, gas, germs. I reckon for poor old Jeb you could add a fourth G for grief which kept him a sort of prisoner for the rest of his days. Daddy went over near the beginning of our involvement, April 1917. It wasn't but a year later we got news daddy's outfit was gassed. It was bad, daddy and some of his company survived long enough to be taken to a field hospital only to pass soon thereafter. I guess at least he didn't pass on the battlefield, maybe he heard the kind voice of a nurse and they had something to help lessen the pain. That's what momma hoped.

1918, yes that's when it began. First daddy to gas, then the so-called "Spanish Flu," what dropped Beau. My first pandemic, 102 years ago, as I say I was eight years old. Started sometime, somewhere in the spring of 1918 rode roughshod over the whole world clear through the spring some say summer of 1919. I guess depending on how you define the beginning and end of such a beast. And it did seem a beast to me, some mysterious invisible beast that took lives willy nilly. I lost an aunt and a couple of uncles, three cousins, countless playmates. I remember the heat that summer, and not being allowed to swim in the local water tank to cool down. Well, we were encouraged to be outdoors, there was a theory that fresh air could help prevent and also help with the cure, but we had to take it by turns. When you are eight it just isn't as much fun alone in that water tank.

We had a service banner with a gold star surrounded by a blue border for daddy, and five blue stars for all but Beau. We hadn't received his yet as he was a recent enlistee. Beau didn't die in battle or on foreign soil so momma wasn't sure if we could put up a second gold star on our service flag, but since he hadn't served yet and didn't die in battle, she didn't think it was right. Several people told her since he was serving in the military when he passed, he deserved a gold star. I thought she should just contact the service flag people and ask. In the end we ended up with enough of those gold stars for any family by the end of the pandemic and the war. Five in all. Would have been six if you count young Beau.

We weren't the only house with service flags, then a new sort of banner started to appear. White scarfs appeared on doors in our neighborhood. We saw that white scarf and knew someone in that house, a neighbor maybe more than one had contracted the flu. We'd hold our breath hoping not to see Doc Homer's hearse, nor a wagon carrying a coffin. Seemed not a day went by when we saw at least one coffin, sometimes more heading out to the cemetery.

I kept asking momma when I was gonna get it. She just looked at me and squeezed her eyes shut then squeezed me and gave me about a billion kisses, then petting my head "Martha Rae, don't talk like that please Martha Rae, don't, don't, don't." Of course, she wouldn't let me out of the house at first, then finally relented so I could cool off in whatever breeze might be on offer on the porch and sometimes later on we'd go to that water tank to take our turn.

I never married. Came close once. Walker Cole Brodey. We planned to be married since we were 7. Through school and all, that never changed. Just got delayed. Walker had a yen to fly so off he went to train. We were going to marry when he got back, but then things changed. He had a chance to join the Flying Tigers over in China, then when Pearl Harbor happened, he got absorbed into the Air Force.

Meanwhile, I became a Rosie. First and only time I left momma. She was so blamed mad about that sneak attack that she wanted to join me. I reminded her about her poor hands near crippled with Dupuytren's contracture and persuaded her someone needed to stay home. I landed training and a job at the Naval Airbase out Corpus Christi way. I roomed with three others, a mother and her two daughters. They helped me with coveralls and boots and how to keep my hair clean out of the way. Cut it right close they did then wrapped a bandana around it. Real cute I thought. It was hard work at first as a trainee, but soon I had muscles like a boy, and later like a man! Some of the women tried to hide their muscles always wearing long sleeves. Not me, I rolled up my sleeves, those muscles were a badge of honor to me. Had a picture taken for Walker. I guess he carried it with him and shared it with his mates proudly. Momma sent us all kinds of home cooked food; she was so grateful to my roommates who really helped me settle to the work. Once I had the training, plus some little tricks you only learn by doing that other women were only too happy to share I took to it like a duck to water.

Our wedding was put on hold that's three times, we didn't mind that we were considered old by that time, I wanted Walker to have his dream, then we'd have plenty of time together to the end of our days. Three times was not the charm for us though. We never did marry.

Momma lived to see the end of WWII. You might say that she was a victim of that fourth G, grief. She was strong and resilient but who can go unwounded with the loss of your husband, all but one of your six children. I think as long as I needed tending to, she was determined to stick it. Plus, she was healthy as a horse. Never once went to the doctor nor needed to. No, I think that last straw for momma was Walker. My beau, my fiancée. Momma always loved that boy, Norma, momma's best lifelong friend's only son. Walker he was sorely wounded late in the war. He made it home, me and Norma and Lee, his daddy, and momma at least we had a chance to say goodbye. He didn't last more than a week though. Momma helped Norma change the blue star on their Service Flag to gold and after that it was like all the strength went out of her. She sat out, right here on this porch every day and rocked and rocked. Just staring. It was all I could do to get her to eat something every day and kept a fresh iced tea with lemon by her side. She barely spoke. Still always had a smile for callers, but her voice was weak. One morning, she just didn't wake up. I've been here alone ever since. I had no interest in any other boy but Walker. He was the one and only for me.

My friend Willa lived across the street. Our mothers were great friends and couldn't keep from talking to one another. Yelling across the street from their porches was more accurate. Willa and I played long distance checkers. We each had the same checkerboard, the only one Dwayne's Five and Dime carried. Red and black checkerboard and red and black pieces. We agreed on splitting the board, Martha Rae's side and Willa's side with numbered columns left to right up to the middle of the board. The rows were lettered from bottom to middle. Each side had our name, so the closest, far left, black space on my side of the board we'd call Martha Rae's A1. Checkers we just identified by their starting place to end place. It worked out real well and helped pass the time. We usually played mid-day so neither one of us would be in full direct sun sweltering away with the other sitting in a nice bit of shade.

Today Bud Tate lives across the street. He and I also play checkers together. Bud sits there with a kitchen towel handy to wipe his brow and yells over "Hoooo EEEE! Hot enough for ya there Mizz Martha?" "Bud Tate, how many times to I have to tell you, you make me feel old when you call me that. It's Martha or Martha Rae. Heat, well yes, it is hot, I'll grant you that, but you know me I like the heat, so it doesn't get me so bad." Fact is I keep my sweater handy even in this heat. Just in case. Nights here can really cool off. Bud tells me I need a metabolism. Sometimes we eat our lunch out there while we play. Once it gets too hot for Bud, we call it a day, leave the pieces where they are. Once bud got a new set from his grandkids, the checkers were all shiny, fake bronze and fake silver but he had to stop using it outside. Our crows and jackdaws being partial to shiny things discovered it one day and he lost a couple shiny checkers…I saw it happen sitting here rocking. Bud and me got a good laugh out of it.

When it gets too hot for the front porch and I still want to be outside I go around back. I usually have a jigsaw puzzle going out there on the screened in porch. I do miss having to pick up pieces that have been swished onto the floor by cats' tails. Get a nice breeze and if there is no breeze, I had a ceiling fan installed several years back.

I still go out for a walk every day, either in the cool of the morning, or that lovely time near dusk, the air still carries the smell of sun and warmth, but we usually get a breeze and as I say I'm less bothered by the heat than most. I carry my mask, around my neck but usually when we neighbors see each other coming, we cross the street or step well up onto someone's yard as we bid hello which usually consists of a nod with a raised hand and we quietly say their name.

"Bud"
"Martha Rae"

"Anna Lu, Rupe"
"Martha Rae"

Sometimes it goes like this.

"Why Winnie good to see you out, your knee?"
"Fine, fine, Martha Rae. Much better today Thank you."

If its tight quarters, we put our masks on.

Every other day I sew a mask or two, my hands can't do it every day. I use some of our heirloom linens that were so nice we never used. Leave a little pocket in them so folks can add filters if they want. Clarie, she's the postmistress, picks them up from my front porch when I have about a dozen or so. She takes care of sending them where most needed. Got the nicest thank you card the other day from a team of retired nurses returned to work up north, it had a photo of them standing outside the blue tent at the hospital they were working out of, spaced out in kind of a W shape to get them all in maintaining distance each wearing one of my masks. Couldn't see much but their eyes which all seemed to be smiling at me right here in my rocking chair. Yes, I had a good healthy cry over that. I'll ask Ronnie to frame it for me, he likes doing little things like that for his "Mizz Martha."

Training Wheels

Red! Of course, red was the color of my tricycle. I think it was a Radio Flyer, but it could have been a Murray. I don't really remember the brand. I remember it was red with white details. I remember the fun. I remember the breath of independence, strength, freedom. I remember the power of my own little feet and legs pumping away at the pedals which turned into wheel-spinning, forward motion. It had a running board between the two back wheels that you could stand on or put one foot on and paddle with the other foot to give a friend a ride or an assist.

When we moved to the 6th Street house I got my first bicycle. It came with training wheels and I bought streamers for the handlebars at Swain's. I'm not sure about the color. It may have been pink with white detailing. I wasn't a big fan of the training wheels. I felt they got in the way more than provided anything. They made the bike feel rickety, unbalanced and not safe. So, one cool gray morning, I put on my favorite jacket, got my bike out of the garage and proceeded to pull tools out of my dad's tool box one or two at a time until I found something that would work, and proceeded to remove the training wheels. I don't remember how old I was. I was pretty little but determined. I guess I'd been far too quiet because eventually mom came out to find out what I was doing. Well, the deed was done. Who knows what kind of mom-worry was going through her head, but there was also a look of pride. I think she helped me put the tools away and we put the training wheels somewhere in the garage, never to be seen again.

Mom watched as I took my first "real" bicycle ride down our gravel driveway, down its slope onto the pavement of 6th Street. Oddly I don't remember that first ride as much as I remember figuring out how to remove the offending training wheels.

One spring I outgrew the little bike and my big sister, Donna, aka "Little Mommy" let me ride her bike when she wasn't using it. It was a Schwinn, blue and white, with a two-tone seat mirroring the color scheme. It may have been a Fair Lady, Tornado or Traveler. I like to think it was a Traveler but I'm not certain. To me, it had all kinds of things going for it: it was my big sister's bike, it was huge compared to my little bike, this bike meant business and I loved the blue and white seat. It said "Climb aboard, sit down and pedal! We got places to go, things to see!" Which I did. All over Port Angeles. It was probably a bit big for me and at first, I had trouble pedaling up the slope of our gravel driveway to get home but that didn't matter. I was riding a "big girl" bike and going places. I sometimes wonder if there were times my sister would have preferred to ride it, but she let me take it out instead. Probably.

That Christmas Eve, a white Christmas as they often were, we set out homemade cookies, homemade fudge and a glass of milk on the fireplace hearth for Santa Claus and took our annual Christmas Eve drive all around Port Angeles to view the Christmas lights. Mom or dad always seemed to forget something and had to run back into the house while the other three of us waited in the heated car. Upon our return, mom or dad would go in first to check that "Santa had been there, eaten his treats and gone..." and plug the tree lights back in. Given the "all clear," we scrambled out of the car and ran into the living room.

Standing next to the tree was a sight that, even thinking about it today, spreads a huge grin across my face. A brand new shiny black with white detail Raleigh 3-speed bicycle. She was sleek, my first bike with gears, lightweight and mine! I particularly loved the two-tone rear fender, black up top, white curving down over the rear tire with the Raleigh emblem. I immediately began putting miles on her. Since it was dark outside and the ground covered in snow, these were indoor miles. Up and down the hallway I don't know how many times. Grinning from ear to ear, laughing and sometimes choking down tears of utter surprise and joy. I continued to ride this bike inside daily until the snow melted and the streets cleared up. Then there was no stopping me! I rode out to my friend's house just on the edge of town, I rode to the YMCA, the park, the library, in the spring I rode to tennis lessons. Mostly though, I just rode with no destination or plan. A ride on this bike was the one guaranteè to put a smile one my face and bring me joy. She grew with me, moved to Anchorage, Alaska with us and moved back to Washington state with us. I still love this bike although I don't know where she is now, she is the litmus test for bikes and bike fit even today.

It was a sad day when I had to admit I had outgrown this bike. In fact, I took a hiatus from bicycle riding. Running and motorcycle riding were my new sources of joy. Alas, one day on my way home from work on the motorcycle, I was hit by a car turning left...the classic crash. Lucky for me I had noticed the oncoming car's front wheels start to turn, straighten, start to turn so I was clued into an indecisive driver who might do anything. This gave me time to re-confirm all possible escape routes (I am a believer in SIPDE: scan, identify, predict, decide and execute). There was still no other traffic. At the last minute the little white Honda Civic did indeed make a mad dash left turn...one of those that I call the "Oh, I COULDA made it" after thoughts that turns into someone executing a maneuver much too late. Anyway, I banged on the left handlebar getting the bike to go left as swiftly as possible—remember no other traffic so this was safe. I managed to only be side-swiped and didn't go down, but my right leg was slammed between the right rear quarter panel and the kick-starter and engine of my bike. My right fibula and tibia were well and truly broken just above the ankle, however, I was elated that there was no damage to the bike. Well, that is a whole different story. How it relates here is that I spent nine months in a cast.

When I was still a few months out from getting the cast off, I asked my orthopedic surgeon about getting strength back as he warned me about muscle atrophy. Could I start running again? He gave me his classic look: he pulled his glasses down his nose and looked over the top of them directly into my eyes and said "Noooo...the best thing for you to do is ride your bicycle." Well at this time I had no bicycle so, of course, I went shopping!

Buying a bike when you are wearing a full-length leg cast and using crutches is a bad idea.

Of course, I didn't think so at the time and I bought a slightly used, fully refurbished silver Cadre Allege Peugeot road bike. I loved the looks of this bike. I loved the idea of this bike. Unfortunately, when the cast was off, and I started to ride this bike none of the "Raleigh magic" was there. Much as I wanted to, I never loved this bike. It was a wonderful bike, just not the bike for me.

First, it was too big. I will never buy a bike when I cannot actually sit on it and ride it again. I stubbornly kept riding anyway. Second, I don't know what it was, but I seemed to get a flat just about every time I went out riding. Riding was not the same experience I remembered with my Raleigh. Still I kept at it, at least until I COULD run again and had strength in my leg to ride my motorcycle again.

One day, I must have been remembering my Raleigh and wanted to ride my bicycle, but I just couldn't get myself out on the Peugeot. So off we went to purchase a new bike.

I found joy again with my sage green Trek Multitrack 720. We began bringing our bikes along on our annual trips to Ashland, Oregon and would ride the Bear Creek Greenway bike and pedestrian trail.

I loved pedaling along next to Bear Creek and looking up at the hills and, after a rather long ride, stopping in at Standing Stone Brewery for a spicy ginger lemonade and pita platter, or, when they were still in business, stopping at Munchie's for a half a BLTA with salad and a piece of the world's best ever strawberry rhubarb pie.

One year I was struggling with some back trouble and had had some wrist/hand/elbow surgeries and I just couldn't get comfortable on my sage green Trek anymore. We stopped off at Ashland Cycle Sport on Oak Street. These guys refit the bike, set me up with new grips and seat all at a reasonable price. As soon as they were done, we headed for the Bear Creek Greenway and there it was, the old "Raleigh grin". I'm forever grateful for these folks for giving me my bicycling joy back.

Fast-forward a few more years. On our annual trip to Ashland, we did a great ride on the way down: The Hiawatha rails to trails ride, which I'll do again and highly recommend by the way, but I was pretty beat up by the end of the ride. I was now dealing with knee trouble and more surgeries on elbow/hand/thumb.

Once in Ashland, we went back to Ashland Cycle Shop and this time I told them my issues, what worked with my Trek and what I felt I needed from it that I wasn't getting.

They fit me out with a 2017 Trek Neko 2 with shocks, disc brakes, more gears and different gearing. I chose Crystal white. The day it arrived and I went to ride it the 4 miles home (we had by this time moved to Ashland) I instantly got my "Raleigh grin" and bicycling joy back. I love my new bike and when I do get out to ride (we are still unpacking and my knee is flaring up, so this is not as often as I'd like) I relax, I laugh, I smile, I breathe.

One day I was feeling pretty "hang-dog." I was having a battle with the blues. I went out for a ride on my bike. In spite of those blues, my "Raleigh grin" appeared, my shoulders relaxed, I breathed. There is nothing like a bike ride to cure high anxiety and low confidence.

Finding Community at the Motor Hotel

I love the community that can be found far from home at the old-style motel. I'm speaking of a true motor hotel where you drive up to the door of your room which may be a cabin attached or detached. It likely has a porch with chairs or benches outside your door with a row of hollyhocks, geraniums and snapdragons blooming. There is no upstairs. There are no long hallways or enclosed spaces. The owners' small children bicycle around the parking lot smiling and speaking to the guests. The guests speak to the guests. Motel room doors are left open and the windows and curtains are opened. Car doors open and close as luggage is brought into the room. People wander out to sit on the porch. A stranger offers another traveler a beer and shares directions to the small market that has some interesting micro brews. Bikers on their way to Sturgis dash over to the on-site laundromat with a handful of clothes; one gets off and lubes his chain. Scientists unload equipment take a bench on the porch and flip open laptops to record and summarize the day and catch up on e-mail before dinner. The scientists are from all over: Purdue, LSU, U of Arizona...brought together on a NASA-funded research project. The motorcyclists are from all over converging on this spot—serendipity of the junction of one of many routes and day's end. Others from as far apart as Delaware and Washington passing through for their own reasons.

We recognize each other at the nearby diner and smile, even say "hello".

In the morning, the scientists are having a meeting in the parking lot under the morning sun. One slips the grey tabby cat a piece of bagel with cream cheese. The lone bikers pack up and motor off one by one, the groups converge with their own meeting while their bikes warm up—route planning, who leads today...

The children are again circling the parking lot on their little bicycles. One speaks to the cat.

"Is that your kitty?"

"Oh, nooooo...that is my GRANDmother's kitty."

"What is the kitty's name."

"DK Kitty, but we call him DK."

The cat settles down in the middle of the parking lot and cleans his paws in the sun.

The term 'motel' was coined in 1925 when Arthur Heineman could not fit the words "Milestone Motor Hotel" on his rooftop so his sign read "Milestone Mo-Tel". Motels can trace their lineage from auto camps and auto courts. Separate cabins became adjacent rooms under one roof, and they continued morphing into what we more commonly think of today in terms of big chain motels where everyone remains a stranger. It is a great treat to get the chance to stay a night in one of these old-style motor hotels. You'll typically get wi-fi along with a hand hooked doily on the table by the bed. Your room may hold the warmth of lamplight against 12" hardwood walls, and as you drop off to sleep, you may feel comfort and kinship about your neighbors for the night.

The Moms

I remember them in their dresses sitting on blankets rumpled by the shape of the ground and grass underneath. Sitting "side-saddle" one hip on the ground, their stockinged legs off to one side, wearing their pumps, open-toed. Smiling, chatting, laughing. Occasionally one would look up and shade her eyes from the sun with her hand, palm out. We, the kids, were playing. Sometimes the moms were backlit, depending on where I'd run to and I remember them as a kind of diorama. It is a distinct memory of mom, not as mom, but as a neighbor and friend to other women—other moms who may have shared a lot in common or nothing in common apart from living on this block in this town at this time and having a child or children. This was the Third Street house and summer.

Exit 148

Peggy had a smoker's voice and served your pie with a quip and a laugh. She waltzed the diner serving tables and booths in constant conversation with everybody. I miss Peggy. She served up a lunch called Pie Lover's Special. Half a sandwich, cup of soup (yes, it was real soup made there) or small salad, and a piece of pie (also made there). I can't think of a more perfect offering on a menu. Perfect road trip fare. Peggy's was the kind of place where regulars and newcomers could all join in the same conversation kept going by Peggy. Made you feel kinda at home even though you were on the road headed someplace else. Yep. I miss Peggy, her constant motion with quips over her shoulder, and her diner too.

Miscellany

Wounded Bird

There is a bird that stands outside the door
On one leg
It is the only leg he has
Somebody ate the other leg
Crunch, crunch, crunch
Probably disappointed not to have acquired the other leg,
Wings too,
And the whole rest of the bird
But the wings of the bird were flapping and powerful
Slapping somebody in the face
And lofting the bird into the air
An escape
Sans one leg
But oh well
Flight, blessed flight
A celebratory call
The bird circles above his would-be captor and diner
Before heading to his nest up in the craggy tree
On the craggy hill
Where he could sun himself and rest

We who were 18

We who were 15
Who followed Woodstock
Or made the journey
And sat in the rain and mud
For music and freedom and community
For three days of peace and music

We who were 15
Who followed Woodstock
Who quietly wanted to go
But lacked one thing or two
To make it happen

We who were 15
Who wove tiny bells into our braids
And played Bob Dylan songs on our guitars
Or tried
Our mouth harp mounted around our necks
"It's alright ma"

We who were 16
Who skipped school to cross the bridge
To march against the Vietnam War
And have our ideals dashed by the violence
Marching for peace in a throng breaking windows
And fighting in Seattle

We who were 16
And saw news crews with their cameras

And realized we shouldn't have worn our
Unique green coat
Who feared being spotted by our parents
Good people watching the evening news

We who were 18
Now armed
With voter registration cards
Proudly displayed in our wallets
Opposite our driver's license
Certain we would make the difference in 1972

We who were 18
We are still 15 and 16 and 18
Who still have hopes and dreams
Who want three days of peace and music and more
And are certain we will make the difference

Wall of Relevance

If you happen upon the Wall of Relevance
What will you find?

If you happen upon the Wall of Relevance
Whom?

What color do you think it will be?
How high? How sound?
How ancient?

Is it warm, even hot, from the startling sun?
Smooth?
Do you want to lean against it to collect its warmth?
Are you alone?

Is it cool, even cold from rain?
Is it stone?
Is it showing its colors that are hidden except when wet?
Do lights reflect off of it and sting your eyes?

Is it weary?
Lonely?

Or has it many fine memories?
Polished from caresses
Wearing its graffiti with grand eloquence

The Dancer's Shoes

There was something sad about that pair of black heels
on the shoe repair counter
with their untied round laces creased and bent
from their long hours of being tied in bows
and a double knot by a woman's hands.
From the size and style of shoe,
pale and shapely hands with slim fingers,
French nails, delicate, in a way, vulnerable hands.
The upper of the shoe almost a velvet
with smooth leather caps and heels.
Almost like a dancer's high heel shoe,
Maybe they had a tap on the bottom of the heel.
Like a 1930s dancer's high heel shoe.
Waiting to be renewed.
I can see her hands
Lacing and tying up the shoe on her high arched foot,
The nicely formed ankle,
The folded form bent gracefully to the task
Blonde hair covering her profile.
Hiding the weary hopefulness of her face.

The Best Loud Child

The best loud child in the grocery store
The produce aisle
We were many, we post-work
Tired hungry just-wanna-buy-something-and-get-home-to-eat
masses
We were in each other's way
Or we weren't really there at all
Or "they" were "they"
Or not there at all

We were many and tired with our grim looks
Our work serious frowns
Our one more item from the checklist
Next line of the program autopilot workweek evening shoppers

Then came the parent
A dreaded loud child in one more cart too many
The child humming
LOUDLY!
You could feel the shoulders tighten
The dread, the get-it-out-of-here vibe
We who were already jostling for the best red pepper
The ripe but not-yet-guacamole avocado
Maybe just space in front of the onions

Then, then it started a holler
This child
More of a sing-shout

This loud child call
"Happy! Happy! Happy! Happy! Happy!"

Singsong on and on but not monotonous
A chant but not hypnotic
Loud but not ponderous
"Happy! Happy! Happy! Happy! Happy!"

We paused
We grinned
We slowly looked up
We looked at this most excellent loud child
A child with wild curly red hair
We smiled
We looked at each other and we were "we" not "they"

Our shoulders dropped, our faces unleashed frowns
The produce was plenty, and we flowed
We passed a bag, a piece of fruit
We turned to make space in front of the onions

"Happy! Happy! Happy! Happy! Happy!"
Sang this best loud child
We smiled at the mother
We made our silly adult faces of encouragement to this child
Exquisite loud child

Ava

Accessibility conference over
Ava and I checking in for return flight home
It has been a good morning
Ava, pierce-tongued, talking about diving
And learning Portuguese
The woman at the airline counter
Looks at me not Ava
Not her white cane
Not her imperfect eyes

She looks at me and asks
"Does she have any luggage to check"
But "she" is right here
I look at Ava
I look at the person at the counter
"I don't know."
I look at Ava
"Ava, do you have any luggage to check?"
I look at the person at the counter
Baffled
Yet now I know why sometimes
Ava is angry

Man Akimbo

Everything about him was loose
His pants were loose
Not baggy, not falling down,
Just well, loose.
His pale blue shirt, too,
Voluminous and billowing
All akimbo to the billowing sandstone colored pants
And his walk was loose and voluminous
And yes, billowing.
Each leg had its own way of walking
It was fortunate that they seemed
To be bound in the same direction
At least roughly speaking.
His arms seemed to be swinging
To a shuck and jive rhythm.
He was a big man too,
Not overweight just big
Which added contrast to the looseness.
Also, his clothes seemed beautifully suited to the desert
Not this Pacific NW rain.
I don't know where he was going.

Melancholy

Why did that word come to mind? Does it matter?
It felt comfortable.
My shoulders relaxed. I was able to accept and even welcome it.
A nuance.
I could smile and enjoy preparing dinner with my melancholy and
my music.

Interpretation has changed over the centuries.
I run to Dürer and the 1500s, *Melancolia I*, and the state of
waiting for inspiration to strike. There is anticipation therein and
hope therefor and therefore.

Imagination, reason and spirit.

Comfort in the grey bluster of rain and wind
which may usher in a clearing and the sun or later,
the moon or stars or satellites.

A hope, a promise, a possibility, a dream, an optimism,
not a leap more a demi plié maybe even a petit jeté of faith.

Let the rain muffle the sounds of the mundane,
the garbage bin, the car alarm, the lowering flaps of the incoming
jet full of people
coming home, visiting, passing through.

Jaape On the Beach, pensive?

The Empty Park

There's something terribly sad about a sun filled park
With nobody in it
No one sunning themselves on the benches dedicated to local
benefactors
No runners
No dogs chasing frisbees
No children on the swings or running round and round to get the
merry-go-round spinning
Serpentine paths with no feet upon them
Grass devoid of blankets or tatami mats or young lovers

Terraform

Willow willow has wept its last
Companions,
Partners in greenery
Gone
Pronounced guilty in the first degree
The claw comes down
Judge jury executioner

Willow willow has wept its last
Not diseased, not yet,
Nor dead, nor rotted
Nor in the way
But for laziness and lack of
Skill Imagination Patience
Ancient growth, beauty
Meaning
Nothing

Willow willow has wept its last
Uprooted by a man sittin' on his ass
Grasped in the claw
Uprooted and shaken to death
To break its neck

Willow willow has wept its last
Companions gone
Willow gone
Leaving mud clay rocks dirt

Severed roots
Scorched earth sans the burn

Willow willow has wept its last
Make way willow for monolith box
Designer bushes, the perfect lawn
Willow willow willow
Gone

New Friend

I have a new friend
In the morning
I walk south
She walks north
In the afternoon
She walks south
I walk north
Lone pedestrians
On the bike/ped trail
It started with a nod
Then
A nod and a smile
A nod a smile a wave
Bigger smiles
A "hi"
A "hello"
A "good morning"
She has dimples like my sister
And a nice smile
We walk the same pace
We don't know each other's name
We may never
Her right hand
Brushes the seed heads
Of the tall grass lining the path
Just
Like
I
Do

Transit Posts

I shared twice daily bus rides with a multitude of humanity. I celebrate my fellows in these Transit Posts.

Grief and Kindness

It was the way the man with you gently stroked your hair back, like stroking a stunned injured bird who has just crashed into a clean window, that caught my attention. I had been reading and looked up only to give my neck some rest. It was beautiful, gentle, one loving stroke from your forehead back then his hand came to rest on his lap. He sat close but not oppressive, letting you know he was there to lean into, cry on, rely on, but giving you space.

Then I saw your black lashes blinking rapidly purposefully and the way you swallowed and pulled your lips in. Holding beautifully erect posture. I sensed you were fighting back tears bearing some kind of gentle sweet quiet grief. Unobtrusively you wiped your right cheekbone with the back of your right hand and did the same on the left leaving a bit of a sheen where a few errant tears had leaked out.

You must have sensed me watching you, I apologize for my intrusion. Lost in your grief but not so lost you couldn't find a kind smile for a stranger.

Brave so brave to be holding it together on the bus. The sobs inside waiting to break free were palpable. I still feel them and am near crying tears for you at the same time I'm grateful for your kind smile.

Early Evening Commute, the 245

Black watch plaid jeans and 4" spike heel suede peach pumps. Sharp. She picked up the woman's cane for her. And then the wraith thin woman with a fever sheen to her face climbed on with heavy luggage. I wondered that she could lift it. She sat and a big shiver wracked her body. She dug out her cell phone and threw one leg atop her bag.

The college student was curled up in as fetal position as possible on a bus. Jungle red nails at the ends of her small delicate fingers. Her black knit watch cap implored "Love Me". She had a little pout painted red.

Morning Observations on the 255

Scored one of the last few high seats
My bench-mate's feet swung free
White leather thongs
Celeste blue toenails
This, a busier route than my 245
Our backpacks and briefcases
Perched on our laps
We don't have the luxury
Of allowing them their own seat
The morning sun filters in
Lighting a chin of the one
In the dragon tee
Lighting a forehead of another
Across the aisle
With his Beats and his music
Nooks, Kindles, iPads, phones
The crackle of a couple of
Good…Old-fashioned…Newspapers
Books, and watchers with smiles
With arms crossed bleary-eyed
The straight-ahead stare
The articulated center
Of the bus rotating
Disorienting in my peripheral vision
Contain the last seats to be filled
Lanky boy, world's perfect eating machine
Baggy "trou"
Ball cap pulled down
And a changing of the guard

At the transit center
The girl sits down on the flare of my skirt
And thumbs still poised over his phone
One man sleeps
And Beats person reads the newspaper
Over another man's shoulder
And one man standing
And now I watch the lake
The couple across from me
Release hands as he gets up
For his stop near downtown REI
She still smiles
Now holding her own hands
On her lap as we pass into the
Dark of the tunnel

Little Hands On the 245

Little hands hang
On the window seal
Face against the glass
Head turning
Laughing pointing
Smiling with joy and speaking her
Own

Special

Language

The world goes by the window
Of the 245
And it is
Wonderful

Metro Mani

She walked right out of the set
Of a 1960's horror flick
You know
The lithe wispy blonde
Wearing a mint dress as light and flowing as a negligee
The type directors always awaken
On a dark and stormy night
Then, send her not out
Not to secure the doors
Grab some hairspray or
Something to cosh the intruder with
Or call for help
But up, up the stairs
Never go up
Don't they know by now?
She walked right up to
Bus stop #72015
She stopped at the route sign
Her dress continued to billow and flow
As she set her pink nail polish on the sign
And proceeded to paint her nails
As she waited for the bus

The 238, Winter Morning

Hybrid sparkling new and quiet
Pulls into Transit Center Bay 4
In the early dawn
Cold
Lights like chandeliers
Sparkle the interior
Pneumatic puff as the doors open
Into the cold they descend
Woven scents of soaps
From all the morning showers
Step down off the bus and hang in the air

Kids from the College

Energy bars
Odwalla drinks
And bloodshot eyes
Maybe catch a few winks

Mom Had Alzheimer's

These Are Not My Mother's Hands

These are not my mother's hands
These are not my mother's hands
And yet this gesture, this gesture
This gesture captured in honeymoon photographs
Remembered from childhood
Caught unawares these are of my mother

These are not my mother's hands
This parchment skin, the fineness morphed to frailty
No these are not my mother's hands which built furniture
Upholstered it, demolished a tree trunk,
Repaired a sewing machine
Strong and yet fine, the hands of the young photojournalist
Who didn't
Because she wanted more to be a mother

These are not my mother's hands
And yet this repose
This shape and curl of the fingers and thumb at rest
The bump in the palm
These are of my mother

These are not my mother's hands
The hands of the woman who has lost her speech
The hands of the woman who may not know me
And yet, the movement, the tenderness

The shape and gesture
Reaching
Reaching out to part my hair on the left
That, that was my mother's hand

We Lost Her Twice

We lost her twice
The first loss perhaps the worst loss
The fear, the puzzlement
Seeking a home sixty years gone

Her momma will be worried

And who are these strangers?
We are eating her cookies
Who are these strangers and what are they doing here?
We are eating her cookies and crying

Reassurance not reassuring
Logic has no place
We drive, we drive her home which is home no more
But the drive seems to bring a temporary calm

Her momma will be worried

He sees his love who sees a stranger
He sees his love looking back in fear
We see our mother who has no daughters
We see our mother lost seeking her own

Her momma will be worried

We hear our mother asking us who we are
We are eating her cookies

We hear our mother asking us to leave this house
We strangers who have eaten her cookies

We lost her twice
We ate her cookies and cried
Six long years
Then the pneumonia, the fever

Her momma will be worried
And we've lost her twice

April Sang to Her

April sang to her
To mom
Silent mom
Here but not here mom
April sang a Christmas carol
Mom's face relaxed
Her eyes, her eyes focused and gathered
Someplace
She quietly smiled
Mom's voice quietly whispered
A faint song remembered
A voice
A joining
A moment of memory
And presence
And Christmas joy

Mom's Fingernails

Thumbnail rubs fingernail
Of "ring finger"
Is it the fourth or third finger?
Either depending on how one counts
There is almost no sound
As these nails are soft, shredded, short
This is my mother's action
That made the clicking sounds
When her hands were idle,
Her "at rest"
The ellipse of arched thumb
Meeting arched fingers poised just above the lap
Her nails were strong and nicely long
Not "Cruella" long
One was longer always
It grew apace
The little finger of
I know not which hand
Unpainted and lovely

The Day That She Knew Me

That day I knew she knew me!

A visit

One of many
Expectations? None
My hair though,
I had changed my hair.
My hair that was kept long as a child
Brushed as a child
Carefully parted as a child
On the left
There is no other memory like that
Of a mom
Brushing one's hair
I hadn't thought about it
Don't know why but that day
That day I had parted my hair on the right.
She was in a chair
I knelt down to look at her face

To put my hand on her hand

A touch
Her eyes
Her eyes changed ever so slightly
She leaned in imperceptibly closer
Freed her hand from beneath mine
She always had pretty hands from the back
When you couldn't see the lumpy palm

Graceful fingers
Reached out shakily
The reach, the movement slow
Shaky but sure
I held my breath
Her nails, naturally prettily shaped
Gently gently drew a line at my brow
Then carefully evenly parted my hair
Parted my hair on the left
Then she was gone
Receded, pulled back
Tears
Tears for
That cherished moment
When mom was back and parting my hair

Made in the USA
Coppell, TX
09 December 2020

43954292R00079